W9-APA-957

DISCARD

RUSSIA

MAJOR WORLD NATIONS

RUSSIA

Julian Popescu

CHELSEA HOUSE PUBLISHERS
Philadelphia

FRONTISPIECE: A view of the Kremlin in Moscow.

Chelsea House Publishers
Contributing Author: Jeff Beneke

Copyright © 1999 by Chelsea House Publishers,
a division of Main Line Book Co.
All rights reserved.
Printed and bound in the United States of America.

First Printing

1   3   5   7   9   8   6   4   2

Library of Congress Cataloging-in-Publication Data
Popescu, Julian.
Russia / Julian Popescu.
p.   cm. — (Major world nations)
Originally published: Let's visit the U.S.S.R. London: Burke, 1967.
Includes index.
Summary: Describes Russia from the time it was explored
to its place in the world today.
ISBN 0-7910-4750-4
1. Russia—Description and travel—Juvenile literature.   [1. Russia.]
I. Popescu, Julian. Russia.   II. Title.   III. Series.
DK29.2P67   1997
947—dc21   97-18041
CIP
AC

CONTENTS

FACTS AT A GLANCE

Land and People

Official Name	Russian Federation
Area	6,592,800 square miles (17,075,200 square kilometers)
Population	147.5 million (1997 est.)
Capital	Moscow (population 8.8 million)
Other Major Cities	Saint Petersburg (4.4 million), Novosibirsk (1.4 million), Nizhniy Novgorod (1.4 million)
Languages	Russian; 140 other languages and dialects
Longest Rivers	Lena, Irtysh, Ob, Volga
Religions	Russian Orthodox, Islam, Judaism, Roman Catholicism, Protestantism
Major Ethnic Groups	Russian (81 percent), Tatar (4 percent), Ukrainian (3 percent)
Major Mountain Ranges	Ural, Caucasus, Altai, Khibiny
Inland Seas	Black, Caspian

National Holiday	June 12, Independence Day
Border Countries	Azerbaijan, Belarus, China, Estonia, Finland, Georgia, Kazakstan, North Korea, Latvia, Lithuania, Mongolia, Norway, Poland, Ukraine

Economy

Natural Resources	Oil, natural gas, coal, timber, furs
Chief Exports	Petroleum and petroleum products, natural gas, wood and wood products, metals, chemicals, military manufactures
Chief Imports	Machinery, consumer goods, medicines, meat, grain, sugar, semifinished metal products
Currency	Ruble (1 ruble = 100 kopeks)

Government

Form of Government	Federation
Head of State	President, elected by voters to a four-year term
Head of Government	Prime minister, appointed by president
Legislature	Bicameral Federal Assembly composed of the Council of the Federation (178 members) and State Duma (450 members)
Highest Court	Constitutional Court
Suffrage	Universal at age 18
Political Subdivisions	21 autonomous republics and 68 autonomous territories and regions

HISTORY AT A GLANCE

700 B.C.   The Slavs emerge as a distinct group.

A.D. 780   The Rus Varangians capture all of the Crimea, ruling their empire from Kiev on the Dnieper River.

856   Rurik seizes control of Rus with the aid of his brothers. He dies in 873. Rurik's successors, Oleg and Igor, wage war against the Byzantine Empire.

1054   The Tatars invade and by 1240 have conquered all of Russia. Their reign is marked by extreme brutality.

1147   Trader Yuri Dolgoruky establishes a *krmyl*, or post, on the Moscow River called Moscow and builds the first wooden Kremlin (fortress) in 1156.

1549   Russia's first Zemsky Sobor convenes. Composed of boyars, it elects Ivan IV the first czar, meaning "little father."

1613   The boyars elect 17-year-old Prince Michael Fedorovich Romanov as czar, thus ending the Time of Troubles. The Romanov dynasty is established.

1682–1725 Czar Peter I reigns. Deeply influenced by the West, he attempts to transform his backward country into a modern state, and largely succeeds.

1762–96 Czarina Catherine II reigns. She pursues some reforms and makes Russia a European empire.

1812–14 Napoléon Bonaparte of France invades Russia. He conquers Moscow and nearly topples the Romanov dynasty. Napoléon is eventually defeated, and Aleksandr I enters Paris as victor.

December 1, 1825 Aleksandr I dies, sparking the Decembrist uprising. It is squelched by his reluctant successor, Nicholas I.

March 3, 1861 The serfs are emancipated under Aleksandr II.

1894 Nicholas II assumes the throne at a time of great internal unrest.

1905 Popular uprisings are crushed by the regime. It is the first serious threat to the Romanov dynasty since Napoléon's invasion.

March 8, 1917 Revolution sweeps the capital, renamed Petrograd, but Nicholas II suppresses the uprising two days later. The Duma refuses to disband, and a provisional government is formed.

March 15, 1917	Nicholas II abdicates in his own name and that of his son, Alexis. The Romanov dynasty is ended.
November 6, 1917	Bolshevik forces seize Petrograd as the provisional government under Aleksandr Kerensky flees. Civil war begins.
1922	The Union of Soviet Socialist Republics is founded.
July 6, 1923	The first Soviet constitution is adopted.
January 21, 1924	Lenin, founder of the Soviet Union, dies. Joseph Stalin emerges as leader.
1936	A series of show trials begin against the "Old Bolsheviks." The Great Purge is launched.
December 5, 1936	A new constitution is adopted.
August 23, 1939	The Soviet Union and Nazi Germany sign a pact of nonaggression. It provides for the division of Poland and for Soviet annexation of the Baltic states.
1939–40	The Soviet Union invades and defeats Finland, which had won its freedom from Russia after World War I.
June 22, 1941	Nazi Germany invades Russia, destroying the entire Soviet air force within hours.
1949	The Soviet Union detonates an atomic bomb, making it the second country after the United States to possess the weapon.

March 5, 1953	Joseph Stalin dies and is succeeded by Nikita Khrushchev.
1956	The Soviets suppress a popular uprising in Hungary.
1961	Soviet cosmonaut Yury Gagarin becomes the first person in space.
1964	Nikita Khrushchev is ousted from office and replaced by Leonid Brezhnev.
1968	Warsaw Pact troops crush a popular uprising in Czechoslovakia.
1972	U.S. president Richard M. Nixon visits the Soviet Union. The era of détente begins.
1977	A new constitution is adopted.
1979	The Soviet Union invades Afghanistan to prop up the pro-Soviet regime. Détente ends.
1980–85	Brezhnev dies. The next two Soviet leaders, Yuri Andropov and Konstantin Chernenko, both die shortly after taking office. Mikhail Gorbachev is then elected Soviet leader.
1989	A new popularly elected legislature is formed, giving the people their first opportunity to elect representatives democratically. Reform sweeps society as the Communist party loses almost all credibility. The Communist regimes of Eastern Europe collapse.

January 1990	The Communist party relinquishes its monopoly on power, and a new government is formed with a powerful presidency.
January 1991	The Soviet army begins a crackdown on independence movements in the Baltic states.
June 1991	Boris Yeltsin is elected president of Russia.
August 1991	A group of senior military officers fails in an attempted coup d'état. Gorbachev resigns as general secretary of the Communist party and recommends that its Central Committee be dissolved.
December 1991	The Russian parliament approves President Yeltsin's plan to establish a commonwealth of independent nations open to former components of the Soviet Union. Ukraine and Belarus join Russia as cofounders of the new union. Ten more Soviet republics soon follow. Gorbachev submits his resignation as Soviet president. The Soviet Union effectively ceases to exist.
1992	Russia takes rapid steps toward a market economy, but production and wages decline.
October 3, 1993	An impasse between the executive and legislative branches leads to armed conflict. With support from the military, Yeltsin prevails and immediately bans opposition parties and newspapers.

December 1993	Russians elect a new parliament and approve a new constitution.
1994	Russian troops invade the republic of Chechnya in an effort to halt moves toward independence. War breaks out.
May 1995	An earthquake strikes the island of Sakhalin, killing about 2,000 people.
December 1995	The Communist party gains control of parliament in legislative elections.
July 1996	Boris Yeltsin is reelected president of Russia.
May 1997	Russia concludes a peace treaty with Chechnya. Russia reaches an agreement with NATO that allows NATO to expand into central and eastern Europe.

RUSSIA

A sign of new times: Moscow holiday shoppers in a modern department store, with Christmas greetings in English as well as Russian.

1

Russia and the World

Russia is the largest country in the world, covering nearly 6.6 million square miles (17 million square kilometers). It stretches from eastern Europe to the Pacific Ocean. With a population density of just 22 persons per square mile (9 persons per square kilometer), it is also one of the most sparsely populated countries in the world.

Few countries in the world experienced as much change and turmoil in the 20th century as Russia. The current Russian Federation was not established until December 25, 1991. For most of the 20th century, Russia was the largest and most powerful republic in the Union of Soviet Socialist Republics (USSR), which was commonly referred to as the Soviet Union. All told, the Soviet Union included 15 republics, which were home to more than 100 national groups. As a military and political Goliath, the Soviet Union shared the title of "superpower" with the United States from 1945 until 1991. Relations between the two superpowers, largely antagonistic, were characterized by the term "cold war"—that is, a condition of permanent hostility that did not actually produce shooting ("hot") war between the two sides.

The rapid demise of the Soviet Union in 1991 caught most of the world by surprise, unleashing a process of social, political, and economic transformation that is still a long way from complete. Whether or not that transformation ultimately brings peace and security to the people of Russia remains to be seen.

The Soviet Union was created in 1917 from the ashes of Imperial Russia. Vladimir Lenin and his revolutionary Bolshevik party shook the world by instituting the first Communist state. Lenin and his successors, however, were only the most recent rulers of a land whose recorded history traces back to A.D. 150. Throughout the centuries and through many changes, Russia was a land of social contrasts—rich and poor, landowner and serf, artist and warrior. Ironically, the Soviet Union, which was created to eliminate those contrasts, retained many of the fundamental elements of traditional Russian society.

Under its imperial rulers, who were known as czars (emperors), Russia expanded in every direction. The 19th century, in particular, witnessed the rapid growth of the empire, which acquired, among other regions, all of Siberia. The international community recognized Russia as a major power, yet Russia was rarely seen as a true equal. The French, British, and Germans of the pre-20th century, who believed themselves to be the standard-bearers of Western civilization, considered the Russians neither European nor Asian—and always somehow inferior. Despite producing great writers and composers, such as Fyodor Dostoyevski and Pyotr Tchaikovsky, Imperial Russia felt compelled to import artisans from Italy and shipbuilders from Holland. This helped to instill western Europeans with a generally low regard for their neighbors to the east. The Russian reaction to such real and perceived slights, their persistent desire for military security, and an unwillingness to adopt 19th-century political liberalism further troubled their relations with the West.

After the Revolution of 1917, international tensions increased dramatically as the new Soviet state set out to overturn the world order through the ideology of communism. Following the end of World War II in 1945, the Soviet Union played an even greater global role. Already a major Asian power, the Soviet Union greatly expanded its influence after the war, first in Eastern Europe through the establishment of Communist governments under direct Soviet control—such as in East Germany, Czechoslovakia, Poland, Romania, Bulgaria, and Hungary—and later by supporting pro-Soviet rebel groups throughout the Third World, from the Caribbean to Africa to Asia. The Soviet Union also grew into a world-class military power. Its nuclear force, in particular, endowed the country with the capability to destroy the world and, with the United States, the ability to foster global peace.

Today the remnants of the Soviet Union, and especially the independent republic of Russia, continue to command the attention of the international community both because of the

Mikhail Gorbachev, shown here with Soviet lawmakers, set in motion the process that transformed the Soviet Union and eventually led to its breakup.

enormous changes that have occurred and because of the large amount of uncertainty these nations face. The changes began innocently enough in 1985, when a fairly obscure junior member of the Politburo, the ruling council of the country, emerged as the leader of the Soviet Union. Mikhail Gorbachev—young, educated, and open—set out to reform a country he perceived as growing increasingly weak. He instituted an economic policy known as *perestroika*, or "restructuring," and a social liberalization policy known as *glasnost*, or "openness." He also established new relationships with the Soviet Union's traditional adversaries—the United States, Western Europe, and China. The world recognized Gorbachev's efforts abroad by awarding him the 1990 Nobel Peace Prize.

Gorbachev's reform movement was a mixed blessing for the Soviet Union. People could now speak their minds and openly criticize the government and the ruling Communist party. Not long before, such expressions of opinion would have brought official harassment, arrest, and even imprisonment. It was a new experience for the peoples of the Soviet Union, and most welcomed their new freedoms with gusto.

Much to the reformers' amazement, however, these changes placed the very existence of the Soviet Union in doubt. By late

Gorbachev's reforms brought greater exposure to outside cultural influences like Western music. Here, Soviet fans ply two singers for autographs; the performer on the left, Udo Lindenberg, is from Germany.

1989, the Soviet-allied Communist regimes in Poland, Hungary, Czechoslovakia, East Germany, Bulgaria, and Romania had collapsed under the weight of public outrage, denying the Soviet Union its western empire. Soon many of the ethnic groups living within the Soviet Union itself lashed out at their Russian rulers, and a number of the Soviet Union's republics declared their independence.

What began as an ambitious, yet limited, effort to reform Soviet society from within quickly escalated into chaos and the complete disintegration of a once powerful and feared empire. New leaders stepped forward to carry the transformation well beyond the goals intended by Gorbachev and his supporters. Some of the new countries born amid the collapse of the Soviet Union seem to have adapted quickly to the new world facing them; others, Russia included, have found the road to a more open society to be bumpy and uncertain. Whatever the future brings, the world community continues to watch as one of its giants gropes to find its way, for Russia's fate will almost certainly affect the world well into the 21st century.

A summer scene at the famous country palace of Peter the Great, near Saint Petersburg.

2

Geography and Wildlife

The largest country in the world, Russia covers as much of the earth's surface as Canada and the United States (the second and third largest countries) combined. It covers 11 time zones, reaching from the Baltic Sea in the west to the Bering Sea in the east. Russia is bordered on the west by the Black Sea, Ukraine, Belarus, Latvia, Estonia, Finland, and Norway; on the north by the Arctic Ocean; on the east by the Pacific Ocean; and on the south by North Korea, China, Mongolia, Kazakstan, the Caspian Sea, Azerbaijan, and Georgia. The detached region of Kaliningrad, which is separated from Russia proper by Latvia and Lithuania, shares a border with Poland.

Russia is composed of three very broad geographic regions, each of which has its own substantial differences. One region is the southern border area, which is primarily uplands and mountains. A second region, the area west of the Ural Mountains, known as European Russia, is primarily a rolling plain, punctuated by low hills. The average elevation here is about 600 feet (180 meters). European Russia is where most of the population lives and where most of the major cities—Moscow, Saint Petersburg (known as Leningrad during the Soviet period), and Volgograd—are located. Moscow, the capital, is the largest, with a population of 8.8 million.

The third region is the vast area known as Siberia. With its huge coniferous forests and tundra, Siberia stretches east from the Urals almost to the Pacific Ocean. Siberia is characterized by lowlands in the west, which tend to be very flat and swampy; a slightly more elevated central platform, which is rich in mineral deposits; and the eastern uplands, consisting of mountains and basins. Though completely conquered by the czars in the mid-19th century, Siberia has yet to be truly settled. Most of it is a scarcely populated, barren wasteland in which a steady, biting wind is the only defining characteristic. For the czars, though, it was a route to a warm-water port on the open sea—the Pacific—and a convenient place to send political enemies and common criminals alike. In recent decades, scientists have discovered large amounts of resources, such as natural gas, in the region, giving Siberia renewed importance.

Climate and Vegetation

The climate of Russia is generally harsh, principally because of its high latitude and the absence of warming influences from the Pacific Ocean. There are also few mountain ranges to break the strong currents that sweep down from the north and across Siberia. The winters are long and cold and the summers brief and cool. The Arctic Ocean freezes right up to the coast of northern Russia in the winter. In Saint Petersburg and Moscow, for instance, the average temperature in winter is no more than 7 degrees Fahrenheit (-14 degrees Celsius). In eastern Siberia, winter temperatures reach -60 to -90 degrees F (-50 to -70 degrees C). In summer, temperatures in most major cities are much more pleasant, averaging in the mid- to high 60s F (approximately 18 degrees C) and reaching into the mid-80s F (30 degrees C) farther

Tourists and street vendors alike dress warmly for an April day in Moscow.

south. Annual precipitation in the country is light to moderate, ranging from 12 inches (300 mm) in the interior basins to 32 inches (800 mm) in the western plains, Siberia, and the eastern regions.

Distinct zones of climate and vegetation tend to stretch across the country in an east-west fashion. The northern tundra is a cold, uninhabitable region marked by low brush, bogs that freeze in the winter and fester in the summer, and permafrost— earth that is permanently frozen. The summer months are short and provide only a brief respite from the wind and cold that have made the tundra one of the most inhospitable places on earth.

South of the barren stretches of the tundra lies the northern forest. Although its perimeter is dotted with small clumps of thin trees and shrubs, the land gradually becomes a belt of thick, at times impenetrable, forest of birch, spruce, and pine. Called the taiga, this zone runs from northeastern Europe to the shores of the Pacific Ocean. The forest is so dense and the soil so poor that the area is best known for its hunting, trapping, and exportable timber harvests.

Farther south, the forests of the north are replaced almost entirely by Russia's famous birch trees. Because the trees are shallow rooted and the climate is considerably warmer than in the northern reaches, the soil is much better, though farming is not a major livelihood.

To the south of the forests lies a belt of drier steppe climate. (A steppe is a semiarid plain.) Here the sparse trees are clumped together in groves, and between them are vast expanses of rich, flat land. This earth, mainly in the steppe's northern half, is ideal for farming, and it is here that Russia produces most of its grains—wheat, oat, barley, and rye. However, unlike the North American Midwest, the region sometimes receives little rainfall and can thus be an area of periodic famine.

The Rivers, Lakes, and Seas

Russia is home to tens of thousands of rivers. The most famous are the Volga, 2,293 miles (3,689 kilometers) long; the Dnieper, 1,420 miles (2,285 kilometers) long; and the Don, 1,224 miles (1,969 kilometers) long. The Volga is far and away the longest river in Europe, although it is only the fourth longest in Russia; the longest is the Lena at 2,670 miles (4,296 kilometers). Because the landscape is so static, there is little change over time in the course of the rivers, though they are prone to flooding each spring, when the snows melt in the north.

Many of the rivers flow to inland bodies of water, either to one of the thousands of lakes that are scattered across the country or to the Caspian Sea. The Caspian, which is bordered on the northwest by Russia, is enormous, covering more than 140,000 square miles (362,600 square kilometers).

Because of the general winter climate of Russia, only the rivers in the southwest flow year-round. Elsewhere, the freezing-and-thawing cycle results in ice jams and flooding, making regular passage of ships difficult throughout much of the year.

The Mountains

The mountain ranges that cross Russia include the Valdai Hills, located 200 miles northwest of Moscow, which are the source of the mighty Volga and Dnieper rivers. Far to the east are the Verkhoyansk Mountains of Siberia, which snake their way south from the Laptev Sea. The most important mountain range in Russia, however, is the Urals. The mineral-rich Ural Mountains divide European Russia from Siberia, and they remain the gateway to what most Russians see as their "wild east." The average elevation of the Urals is not especially impressive, being only about 2,000 feet (600 meters). The highest elevation, at 6,214 feet (1,894 meters) is in the north at Gora Narodnaya.

Animal Life

Because Russia extends from the Arctic regions of the north to the southern steppes, the country boasts a fabulous array of animal life. Like the vegetation, the wildlife becomes more plentiful toward the southern regions of the country.

The tundra is home to few animal species. Throughout the year, Arctic foxes and lemmings can be found scurrying about, and the occasional herd of reindeer can be spotted charging across the tundra's hard, cold landscape. The region is also home to the polar bear, seal, walrus, and white hare. When the temperature is somewhat warmer in summer, numerous birds take to the air, including swans, long-tailed ducks, sandpipers, and geese. Moreover, the partially thawed earth releases swarms of gnats that blacken the air around pools of stagnant water.

Farther to the south, the forest springs forth with an abundance of wildlife. In the northern areas of the region are such

Participants prepare their reindeer for a race at the winter festival in Murmansk, the largest city inside the Arctic Circle. In this area of the far north, "night" lasts three weeks at the height of winter, and "day" lasts three weeks in the summer.

beasts as the brown bear, the elk, and the coveted sable. Mouse-like voles, wolverines, and lemmings also can be found. Among the many species of birds are the great gray owl, the woodpecker, and the bullfinch. Farther south in the forest, numerous deer, polecats, and nightingales can be seen. In the southernmost reaches of the region, many of the greatest and most fearsome creatures on earth reside: Black bears, leopards, and tigers stalk the thick woods, wary of no one but the hunters who also ply the dense terrain.

The animals of the steppes are at once plentiful and constantly endangered. Such unique species as the marmot, jerboa, lark, and imperial eagle can be found in relative abundance. In the more eastern regions of the steppes, along the border with Mongolia, gazelle and pika roam freely. Unfortunately, the animal life of the region has been significantly altered over the centuries as a result of increased farming. The wild horse, for example, is now extinct, and many other species have migrated to refuge in the forests of the north.

Perhaps the most abundant variety of wildlife is found in the Caucasus region. Wild boar, mountain goats, chamois, deer, hyena, jackal, porcupine, leopard, and bear inhabit the area, as do such game fowl as turkey, grouse, and partridge. Snakes and lizards are also numerous.

The country's extensive system of rivers, lakes, and seas holds a variety of fish life. Though the waters of the Arctic region are too cold to support many species, sturgeon, carp, and chub abound in the warmer waters of the Caspian and Baltic seas.

Its very size, diverse regions, and climatic extremes make Russia one of the most fascinating and important natural habitats in the world. Several endangered species reside in Russia, including the snow leopard, tiger, short-tailed albatross, and Oriental stork. For this reason, among others, environmental protection in Russia is important for everyone, Russians and foreigners alike.

In 1916, the ballerina Anna Pavlova poses with another dancer. Pavlova studied at the Imperial Ballet School in Saint Petersburg and later became well known for her interpretations of classical roles and particularly for her solo The Dying Swan.

3

Peoples and Cultures

In addition to being the largest country on earth, Russia is culturally one of the most complex. There are more than 100 separate national groups living in Russia, with approximately 140 languages and dialects spoken within its borders.

Both the czarist and Soviet empires, for all their differences, shared in the dominance of the ethnic Russians (or Great Russians). For all of its professed internationalism, the Soviet Union was very much a Russian regime with a distinctly Russian outlook. The challenge to Russian domination by many of the varied ethnic regions played a large part in the Soviet Union's demise. This problem of ethnic separatism has continued within the new nation of Russia. For example, the Chechen rebellion that began in 1994 had a strong ethnic component.

Numerically, Russians accounted for about half of the population within the Soviet Union. Today, in the independent nation of Russia, ethnic Russians constitute 81 percent of the population. Tatars are the largest minority, making up about 4 percent of the population, followed by Ukrainians (3 percent) and Chuvash (1 percent).

The Soviet Union was officially atheist; that is, the state denied

On June 18, 1990, in Saint Petersburg, Russian Orthodox Patriarch Aleksy II leads a service to reopen the Issaski church, which had been closed for more than 50 years. Since the relaxation of state controls in the late 1980s, Russia has experienced a religious resurgence.

the existence of God. This resulted in the closing of places of worship and the persecution of religiously active citizens. The Soviets, however, did allow the practice of religion in many of the non-Russian regions. Islam, in particular, remained a vibrant part of life for the Muslim peoples of Central Asia. With the collapse of the Soviet Union, Russia has experienced something of a religious revival, most of it based on the traditional religions of Orthodox and other forms of Christianity, Islam, Judaism, and Buddhism. An estimated 35 million people are followers of the Russian Orthodox church, and Orthodox holidays are today observed by the government.

Food and Drink

The favored food and drink of Russians tends to vary among ethnic groups. The peoples of Far Asia, for example, rely heavily on fish as a staple because they live close to the sea. In European Russia, bread and potatoes constitute the main dietary staple. Generally, the Russians are not noted for their cuisine. Main courses, such as meat dishes, tend to be heavy, often smothered in creamy sauces. Certain foods, however, are known throughout much of the world, such as black bread and borscht, a thick beet and cabbage soup topped with sour cream. Russian caviar—raw sturgeon eggs—has long been an expensive delicacy and remains a leading export.

Most meals are enjoyed with wine, but because Russian wine tends to be exceedingly sweet, it cannot compete with the more delicate products of France and Italy. Russian vodka, however,

A Moscow woman sinks her teeth into Western-style fast food—one result of increasing trade with the West.

may be the most widely consumed beverage in the nation, and it is eagerly imported by the West. Unfortunately, vodka has also become the bane of a country steeped in alcoholism.

Western foods have begun to have an impact on Russia. As a result of increased trade with the West, fast-food chains such as McDonald's, Pizza Hut, and Ben & Jerry's Ice Cream have been able to introduce uniquely Western foods to the Russian people, first in Moscow and eventually in other major urban centers as well. They have proven to be very popular, though less for their taste than for their novelty.

The Arts

Historically, Russia has made many truly outstanding contributions to intellectual and cultural life. For example, it was during the Byzantine period (988–1530) that icon painting was born. Icons—religious images that adorned Russia's churches, palaces and private homes—became as important a symbol of the devout religious beliefs of Russians as the cross itself. (See the illustration on page 81.) Later, the so-called Novgorod School introduced the magnificent frescoes that to this day make Russia's churches and former royal residences among the world's most beautiful structures.

The 18th and 19th centuries witnessed the influence of Western art on Russian artisans. The course of Russian art during this period had much to do with the individual tastes of the reigning czars and czarinas. When Peter the Great invited western European artisans to help build his new city of Saint Petersburg in the early 1700s, it was, in part, a reflection of the czar's personal prejudices.

French culture had a particularly strong impact on many of Europe's royal houses, and the Russian royalty was not immune. Such Russian artists as Ivan Argunov and Fedor Rokotov, who studied under imported French masters, reflected this influence in their work. Events such as the Napoleonic invasion, however, reinstilled the arts with a sense of Russian nationalism, and subsequent painters, such as Ilya Repin (1844–1930), adopted uniquely Russian themes. Repin's *The Volga Bargemen* is probably the most popular painting of this period.

The late 19th century and the first years of the 20th century witnessed a strong Russian contribution to modern art. The radical movements of modern art, such as Cubism, Expressionism, Constructivism, and Suprematism, were interpreted by many European traditionalists as an implicit endorsement of political radicalism. Indeed, ultramodernist artists such as Ilya Mashkov (1881–1944) and Aleksandr Kuprin (1870–1938) were, at the very least, intellectually sympathetic to the movements of the Left. In Russia, however, modernist artists were often persecuted. The struggle between traditionalism and modernism in Russian art truly reflected the struggles in Russian political life.

Russia developed its own unique style of architecture as well. The history of Russian architecture can be broken into four principal periods—the Byzantine (10th to 16th century), and Muscovite (16th to 18th century), the European (18th to early 20th century), and the Soviet (early 20th century to 1991).

The Byzantine period reflected the styles of eastern Europe. This was most noticeable in the construction of churches, because Russia's adoption of Eastern Orthodox Christianity during this period translated into the architecture. The most prominent characteristic of the Byzantine period was the use of onion-shaped domes. Because of the abundance of forests, most of these domes were built of wood and thus have long since vanished.

The Muscovite period marked the emergence of a uniquely Russian form of architectural design. It was during this period that the two most recognizable Russian structures were raised— the Kremlin in Moscow and the Cathedral of St. Basil the Blessed (now called the Cathedral of the Intercession) outside its gates. The Kremlin was originally a walled wooden fortress used to protect traders in an untamed land. Between 1475 and 1510, Italian artisans were hired to create a more permanent Kremlin after the original had burned. Located in the middle of Moscow, the Kremlin contains three churches and several palaces. Once the home of the monarchy, the Kremlin is today the seat of the government and the center of the Russian Orthodox church.

Close by the Kremlin, the Cathedral of St. Basil the Blessed was erected between 1555 and 1560. Fashioned in masonry after the style of the wooden churches of the Byzantine period, it is adorned in bright, contrasting colors and is one of the most visually spectacular structures in the world.

The European period reflected the czars' and czarinas' taste for the western European style of architecture. Such grandiose works as Peter I's Winter Palace in Saint Petersburg, Catherine's Palace outside Moscow, and the Bolshoi Theater in Moscow are akin to Western residences, government buildings, and public

Within the red brick walls of the Kremlin—the oldest section of Moscow—stand the Bell Tower of Ivan the Great (far right), the cathedrals of the Archangel and the Annunciation (center), and the Grand Kremlin Palace (left), among other buildings.

sites of the same period. Still, they retain a distinctly Russian flavor.

The Soviet period may be more accurately referred to as the Stalinist period. Under the reign of Joseph Stalin (1928–53), the Soviet state undertook enormous construction projects, in part to prove the success of the regime. Determined to break with the past, the Soviets adopted a style they perceived as modern—a style that was, in fact, cold and imposing. Seven large "skyscrapers," with bulky towers and blank facades, long dominated the Moscow skyline. In recent decades the Soviet and Russian governments, moving away from this architectural approach, have begun to work with steel and glass in a style similar to that of Western office buildings. By the mid-1990s, Moscow was in the midst of a large-scale building boom, principally of lavish offices for multinational corporations and fancy mansions for the newly rich.

Musically, Russians have contributed to the arts in numerous ways. Perhaps the music most readily identified with Russia is produced by the balalaika. This six-stringed triangular instrument resembles a guitar but produces a tinnier sound, and even today at least one person who is proficient on the balalaika can be found in almost every Russian village.

Russia can claim many of classical music's leading figures as its own. Pyotr Tchaikovsky and Igor Stravinsky are universally recognized as two of the world's greatest composers, and their instrumental and operatic works continue to thrill audiences around the globe. Even under Soviet rule, Russian orchestras and opera companies ranked among the world's finest.

Russia's tradition of excellence in the field of ballet has been an inspiration to the world. The development of modern Russian ballet can be attributed to Sergey Diaghilev (1872–1929), who founded the Ballets Russes in 1909 and within a few short years gained world acclaim. Upon his death in 1929, Diaghilev was

Composer Igor Stravinsky (left) and dancer-choreographer Vaslav Nijinsky collaborated on the ballet Pétrouchka *in 1911. This work, which was first performed by Nijinsky in Sergey Diaghilev's Ballets Russes, is the tragic story of a puppet endowed with a human heart.*

succeeded by the choreographer George Balanchine, who later immigrated to the United States and established the American School of Ballet and later the New York City Ballet.

Russia's ballet schools, including the Bolshoi in Moscow and the Saint Petersburg (formerly Kirov) Ballet, have consistently produced many of the world's greatest ballet dancers and choreographers. Lev Ivanov, Vaslav Nijinsky, Anna Pavlova, Rudolph Nureyev, and Mikhail Baryshnikov are but a handful of ballet geniuses who have come from the Russian ballet tradition.

Russia's world-renowned museums, such as the Hermitage in Saint Petersburg, provide a vivid look into old Russia. Despite their concerted effort to break with the past, the Soviets took great care to preserve the relics of bygone eras. The trappings of the monarchy—gilded coaches, crown jewels, and elaborate vestments—dazzle museum visitors. Russian museums also provide splendid showcases for the country's extensive collection of priceless artwork.

For those Russians who prefer lighter entertainment, the circus provides a wonderful show. Skilled acrobats, dancing bears, clowns, and musicians continue to thrill audiences. The Moscow Circus, for example, regularly tours the world.

Literature and Theater

Few peoples have made as strong an impact with the written word as the Russians. Russian literature itself can be traced back to the 11th century. From then until the 18th century it possessed a strongly religious theme. As in most of Europe, those people outside the ruling nobility who were literate were religious leaders; understandably, they wrote about what they knew best. At roughly the same time, the Russian parable gained prominence. These light stories, written to impart a meaning to everyday life, were easily understood and widely popular.

It was not until the 19th century, however, that Russian literature fully blossomed. Poetry in particular became an important literary form, and the Russian people's devotion to verse was recognized as a window into the Russian soul. Perhaps the greatest Russian poet was Aleksandr Pushkin (1799–1837). During his brief but rousing lifetime, Pushkin produced many of the world's finest poems. Works such as *Eugene Onegin*, a verse-novel about a shallow, pleasure-loving man's insensitivity toward the love of a noblewoman, displayed a beauty and ability matched by few other poets. Pushkin's ability to capture human sympathy in his characters—most of whom are seen as victims rather than as masters of their own fate—has rarely been equaled.

The 19th century was also a heyday for Russian prose. The first

The writers Lev Tolstoy (left) and Maksim Gorky in 1900. Tolstoy, who was born to a wealthy family, and Gorky, who came from a working-class background, wrote frequently about moral issues and the suffering of the peasants. Both authors were controversial in their time. Tolstoy was excommunicated from the Russian Orthodox church in 1901 for his antireligious views, and Gorky was exiled from Russia after the failure of the 1905 revolution.

great Russian writer of the modern era was Nikolay Gogol (1809–52), and it was he who set the standard for modern Russian literature. Gogol was both a novelist and dramatist, and his works were the first to serve as social commentary. His 1836 play *The Inspector General*, about a small town's reaction to a visiting dignitary, illustrated the absurdity of life under the czars through biting humor. Literature has always been an outlet for social frustrations, but in oppressive Russia it became even more so.

Fyodor Dostoyevski (1821–81) followed Gogol in expressing the inequities and injustices of Russian society through literature, but with a more somber tone. His novels *Crime and Punishment*, *The Possessed*, and *The Brothers Karamazov* sadly described not only the hopelessness and despair but also the everyday conditions of Russian life and the negative impact that those conditions had on common thinking. In the 19th century, Dostoyevski was to Russia what Charles Dickens was to England.

The writings of Lev Tolstoy (1828–1910) also illuminated the plight of the common man. Tolstoy was one of Russia's—and the world's—greatest literary figures. In novels such as *War and Peace* and *Anna Karénina,* he attempted to show how flaws of character led to the horrors of Russian life. Tolstoy's works were ultimately interpreted more as insight into human nature than as social commentary. Nonetheless, his descriptions of Russian society were profound and influential.

Anton Chekhov (1860–1904) and Maksim Gorky (the pen name of Aleksey Peshkov, 1868–1936) illustrate the very different strains in Russian literary life. Chekhov's numerous short stories and plays took a decidedly nonpolitical approach, and his works were hailed not as social commentary but as pure literature and drama. Chekhov was a medical doctor from a relatively prosperous Moscow family who harbored less social outrage than did many of his contemporaries. Gorky, on the other hand, came from a poor background and never forgot the chronic suffering of the peasant class. His plays and poems reflect his political radicalism, and the Soviets presumptuously hailed him as one of their own.

Ivan IV became the first "czar" of Russia in 1549. Though he was an innovative ruler, his tyranny and ruthlessness earned him the nickname Ivan the Terrible.

4

Prerevolutionary Russia

The first people known to have settled the vast land that is now Russia were the Slavs. Because they left no written records behind, it is difficult to pinpoint precisely when they began to settle the region. But it is known that the Slavs were a distinct group by 700 B.C.

As they gained a more permanent foothold in the region and their numbers continued to grow, the Slavs spread out across the wide expanses at their disposal. One group moved westward into what is now Eastern Europe, another headed south into the Balkan mountains, and a third went east into the fertile steppes—they were the predecessors of the Russians and Ukrainians. A small offshoot of this last group, known as the Varangians, moved northward into the thick forests. Each group quickly adapted to its surroundings, either hunting, fishing, trapping, or farming, depending on the quality of the soil and the climate.

In time, the proliferation of different groups led to warfare and the establishment of recognized borders. The Varangians were the first to found a state, which they called Rus, making their capital in Kiev, on the Dnieper River. Soon the Rus Varangians were expanding their territorial holdings and by A.D. 780 had seized all of the Crimea.

In 856 a warrior chief named Rurik emerged. With the aid of his brothers, he seized control of Rus and established a formal Kievan state. Rurik ruled Kiev for 17 years. At his death in 873, his successor, Oleg, assumed control of the burgeoning kingdom. In 907, Oleg attacked Constantinople (the capital of the Byzantine Empire, known today as Istanbul), and his successor, Igor, struck the city again in 944. Kiev had become a credible power by A.D. 1000.

By 1054, however, power struggles and family feuds significantly weakened Rus, to the point where it could effectively defend neither itself nor its trade routes. It was not surprising, then, that by 1240 all of Russia fell to the invading Tatars from the east. The Tatars ruled over their empire with brutality, and their reign left a deep impression on the Slavs.

Not until 1480 would Russia again be free, but in 1147 a seemingly small event occurred that would eventually be of major im-

A 1628 woodcut of the plan of Moscow, founded almost five centuries earlier by the trader Yuri Dolgoruky.

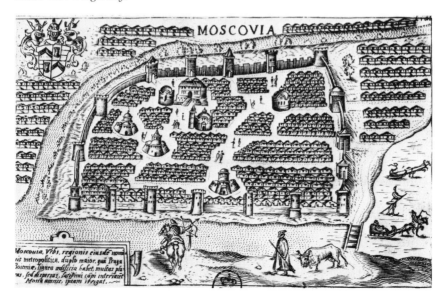

portance to Russia: A trader by the name of Yuri Dolgoruky established a *krmyl*, or post, on the Moscow River, appropriately named Moscow. (The term Kremlin, which comes from the word *krmyl*, refers to the wooden fortress that Dolgoruky built around the settlement in 1156.)

Ivan III

Centrally located on several important trade routes, Moscow rapidly grew into a recognized center of commerce. After being sacked and burned in 1382, Moscow was liberated from the Tatars in 1480 by Prince Ivan III. It soon became the undisputed seat of power in the east. Ivan III, known as Ivan the Great, not only expanded the rule of Moscow through his control of massive armies; he also established the Russian Orthodox church. In 1439 the Greek Orthodox church, which claimed numerous followers across Russia, "unified" with the Roman Catholic church. This union was rejected by many Russians, who believed their crown prince to be the successor to the Byzantine emperors. Through adherence to his own faith and a ready willingness to forge a political bond between the Crown and Russia's religious leaders, Ivan the Great inextricably tied the new church to the throne.

Ivan the Terrible

It was not until 1547 that another grand prince, Ivan IV, took the first steps toward building a true kingdom. When Ivan IV assumed the throne at the age of 16, he inherited a loose federation of divergent ethnic groups. Under the influence of his most prominent subjects—especially those in business, government, and the church—the crown prince instantly recognized that if his rule was to last, he had to transform his domain into a politically unified kingdom. He did so through a combination of political maneuvering and sheer force.

In 1549, Russia's first *Zemsky Sobor*, or "the assembly of the

48

country," convened. Composed of *boyars,* local princely land-owners, the Sobor elected Ivan IV the first czar, which means "lit-tle father" in Russian. Ivan IV quickly used his new powers to further expand the country territorially. In 1558, however, when he sought a port on the Baltic, Russia suffered its first real defeat at the hands of the Poles. This blow, coupled with his insistence that he alone reserved the right to rule, put Ivan IV at odds with the boyars.

Instead of directly confronting his enemies, Ivan IV circum-vented them. He divided all of the land in Russia between the monarchy and the boyars. Then he gave away much of the land that he had claimed for himself, thus creating a new landowning class that owed allegiance to the throne. Soon the traditional economy collapsed, and Ivan IV emerged as the unquestioned authority in Russia.

Ivan IV was one of the most influential figures in Russian his-tory. He was a creative ruler who devised the system of propor-tional taxation and used state funds to support the arts. He hired the country's finest artisans to adorn his palaces and churches with their icons and mosaics. Yet he was also a tyrant who would kill messengers for bringing bad news. He leveled some cities—such as Moscow's rival city, Novgorod—and killed many of their inhabitants. In his mere presence, members of his court and fam-ily would shudder. For whatever good he may have done for Russia, Ivan IV may be best known for murdering his own son in a fit of rage, an act that he regretted for the remainder of his life.

By the end of Ivan IV's reign, Russia had become a land of con-trasts. It was developing faster than had most other states, but it was also becoming increasingly oppressive. Indeed, life became so difficult that refugees regularly fled across the borders to es-cape Ivan the Terrible, as he came to be known.

Perhaps the most distasteful development was the institution of serfdom. The boyars were small kings in their own right, and people who lived under them were at their beck and call. Although many peasants owned small plots of land, many worked on the boyars' vast estates. Heavily taxed, they were unable to pay what they owed their masters, so they had to continue to work, and their debts continued to rise. The serfs were forbidden to leave the estates and so were forever in debt. Their indentured status soon became an institution, and an entire segment of the population in essence became slaves. This state of affairs would haunt Russia for the next two centuries.

The Romanovs

By the early 17th century, Russia had become a major regional power, a change that did not go unnoticed among its more stable neighbors to the west. On September 30, 1610, an invading Polish army entered Moscow, and except for a Russo-Polish treaty supported by the embittered boyars, Russia came perilously close to falling under direct Polish rule. Infighting ensued, and the next three years became known as the Time of Troubles.

In 1613, the boyars finally moved to resolve the lingering crisis: They elected a czar, a 17-year-old prince from among their ranks, Michael Fedorovich Romanov. Michael and his two immediate successors, Alexis and Fedor III, ruled Russia until 1682. Their successive reigns solidified the Romanov dynasty and in the process began to shape Russia the kingdom into Russia the nation. A nominal constitutional monarchy was adopted from the old Moscow state. Officially, power was divided among the Crown, the *Duma* (boyars' council), and the *Sobory* (local land councils). In fact, the Romanov dynasty gradually assumed almost complete control over the country. Its authority was limited only by the sheer size of the kingdom.

The Russian Orthodox church also grew in stature. From the church came the "divine" legitimacy of the throne. Within the church itself, however, a schism opened between reformers, led by Czar Fedor, and the so-called Old Believers, those who remained committed to the original practices of the church. In the long run, it was the Old Believers who most consistently supported the throne.

As a relatively powerful state, Russia under the first Romanovs began to take on greater regional stature. Peace treaties were signed with Poland and Sweden, Russia's historical adversaries. The czars ceded much of their territory in the north, but they were quick to move to the west and south whenever their neighbors appeared weak. At the same time, a small but growing community of foreigners, mainly traders, established themselves in Moscow, and their influence grew steadily. By the mid-17th century, Russia was well on its way to becoming a true power, although it would not become a world-class empire until the 18th century.

Peter the Great

Between 1682 and 1725, Russia underwent a rapid transformation from a land of backward, inward-looking princes and peasants to an emerging political, financial, and military power recognized throughout Europe. This change was largely due to the efforts of one man, Czar Peter I, who would be remembered forever as Peter the Great. A man of keen intellectual powers, Peter was unquestionably the premier authority in Russia, not only because he was the czar, but because his personality, determination, and frequent ruthlessness made him a difficult figure to resist.

Peter the Great's determination to transform his country derived largely from the fact that the young monarch had traveled widely in Europe. Unlike his predecessors, who cared little about how the world worked beyond Russia's borders, Peter yearned to see firsthand exactly what it was that made a great power great. So he set out for the cities of the West in disguise; after all, a czar would be treated as a dignitary, not as a student. Peter's travels took him to many of Europe's great cities, including Am-

Peter I, known as Peter the Great, was determined to make Russia equal to its neighbors in the West. Transforming the country into a modern state, he established Russia as northern Europe's leading military power. He also founded a new capital, Saint Petersburg, which gave Russia an outlet to the Baltic Sea.

PETRUS PRIMUS RUSSORUM IMPERATOR

sterdam, London, and Prague. He saw marketplaces in action, civil servants at work, factories at full capacity, banking institutions in operation, and military machines fitted with modern weapons—and he was impressed.

Back home, Peter immediately set out to make Russia an extension of the West, whether or not his people liked it. Taxes were raised to construct a new capital on the marshy banks of the Baltic, aptly named Saint Petersburg, and Italian artisans were brought in to make this "door to the West" a proud symbol of the new Russia. Textile factories sprang up across the landscape, a civil service was created, and the government was divided into administrative departments. A senate was formed to replace the Duma. The military, especially the navy, was completely reorganized and refitted, and Peter took advantage of these improvements to significantly expand the empire's territorial possessions. The Russian Orthodox church was placed under the direct jurisdiction of the throne through the creation of the Holy Governing Synod, thus stripping the church of its independent authority. Military and technical academies were established as science and engineering began to flourish. And relations with the West were greatly expanded. Peter established formal diplomatic ties with such great powers as England and Holland and encouraged travel and trade between his empire and the developed world. Thanks to Peter the Great, Russia was thrust into the modern age.

The road to modernization under Peter I was by no means easy, and much of the czar's energy was spent on "convincing" his subjects that modernization was in the best interest of the kingdom. An absolute monarch need not use political persuasion to have his way, merely a forceful hand. Peter believed that if Russia was to be modern, then it must look modern—which was largely the rationale for building Saint Petersburg. When members of his court, for example, refused to follow Western fashions by shaving off their beards, Peter had it done for them. He was powerful but not always well liked, and by the end of his reign, Peter's Russia was plagued by regional unrest and peasant revolts.

Over the next two centuries, the Westernization that Peter set in motion had profound consequences for Russian society. Russia became a mix of uniquely Russian interests and practices and an active desire to be "Western." Not only the ruling classes, but also the Russian merchant and industrial classes came to see Western life as a cultural standard. Their children learned French, the "international" language; they eagerly awaited the latest fashions from Paris and London; and they sponsored artists who had adopted Western techniques. They traveled widely and, with their money, extended much of Western society to the far corners of Russia. By the later 1800s each of Russia's major cities had developed a fashion district where nattily dressed men and women strolled the streets. Schools were established to teach young ladies the finer points of high society. Homes were decorated in Victorian style; elegant restaurants staffed French chefs; and orchestra and opera houses were built in the finest of Western traditions.

Catherine the Great

If Peter I set Russia on the path to becoming a modern nation, then it was Catherine II who made it a modern empire. Catherine, born Princess Sophia in Prussia in 1729, assumed the Russian throne in 1762 as the result of the often violent court intrigues. With the help of her supporters, Catherine overthrew her husband, Peter III, and quickly proved herself worthy of the title czarina.

After Peter I's death in 1725, it had become fashionable among his survivors to declare themselves modernizers in his mold, but few could match him either politically or intellectually. Catherine, however, was quite the opposite. A well-read woman who was widely versed in the liberal thinking of the day, Catherine set out to fashion an enlightened reign in which the rule of law dictated policy. She established a parliament representing a cross section of the empire, and she crafted a new legal code. Not surprisingly, the czarina met sharp resistance from the landowning class, which eventually pressured her into relinquishing much of her domestic authority. She did establish a local system of government, though, that lasted well beyond her reign.

Frustrated by the sluggish pace of her reforms at home, Catherine turned her attention to foreign affairs. One of her principal objectives was the conquest and annexation of Russia's traditional enemy, Poland. Through a deft agreement with Prussia in 1772, she managed to absorb the eastern half of Poland, including the city of Warsaw. Catherine's attempt to drive the Turks from the

Catherine II continued Peter I's drive to westernize Russia and add territories to the empire. During her reign, domestic reforms increased the efficiency of provincial administration and improved the nation's banking system. Catherine was also a great patron of musicians, artists, and philosophers of the Enlightenment era.

southern shore of the Black Sea failed despite two wars against the Ottoman Empire, but her overall success in the politics of alliance made Russia a full member of the European community.

Catherine might have gone down in history as an even greater reformer than her predecessor, Peter I, had it not been for developments at the other end of Europe. In 1789 popular revolution swept France, toppling one of the most powerful monarchies in the world. Perhaps it was the specter of a worldwide democratic movement (the Americans had freed themselves from British rule by 1783) that frightened Catherine, or the news that France's King Louis XVI had been publicly beheaded. In any event,

Catherine abandoned her reform movement, and whatever chance there might have been for a constitutional monarchy in Russia came to an end.

When she died in 1796, Catherine the Great left behind a mixed legacy. She had earned Imperial Russia a place among the most powerful countries in the world, and she had introduced several enduring domestic reforms; but she failed to abolish serfdom and to give the kingdom a genuine constitutional system. Little did she know that she may well have set the stage for one of the greatest upheavals in modern history.

Aleksandr the Great

Aleksandr I, Catherine's grandson, was similar to his grandmother in several respects. Intelligent and worldly, the young Aleksandr was Catherine's favorite if for no other reason than that her son—Aleksandr's father, Paul I—was a madman given to fits of rage. After Paul's assassination in 1801, liberal reform once again found encouragement from the throne, and once again Russia was offered the chance to become a truly enlightened monarchy.

Aleksandr I and his private advisory committee, composed of his most trusted allies, set out to establish a permanent rule of law. Serfdom was still the most chronic problem in the realm. In 1803 Aleksandr issued a royal *ukaz*, or edict, giving landowners the right to free their serfs, though few did. A drive was also begun to overhaul the educational system, and three new universities were established. But Aleksandr walked a tightrope between cautious reform and revolution. On one side he had the fiercely reactionary landowners and their church allies; on the other, committed constitutionalists and radicals. He could ill afford to move too far one way or the other.

Aleksandr might have gone down in history as yet another

moderate czar had it not been for French emperor Napoléon Bonaparte's invasion of Russia in 1812. As Napoléon trampled across most of Europe, Aleksandr had tried first to ally Russia with France's enemies and later to ally it with Napoléon himself in an attempt to ward off a French attack. When Napoléon finally turned his massive armies against Russia, Aleksandr found himself swept up in a nationalist furor. Conservatives in Russia disapproved of the czar's ties to Paris and indirectly blamed Aleksandr for the French assault. He could now only foster the nationalism that would help save his kingdom from French rule and his throne from the Russian nobles.

Napoléon's invasion of Russia was one of the most important and devastating events in modern history. French legions laid waste to everything in their path, destroying cities, ravaging crops, and killing thousands. It seemed as if the Russian monarchy were finished when Napoléon triumphantly marched into a burning Moscow and straight into the Kremlin, the czar's Moscow palace. But the freezing weather set in, and Napoléon,

With the Russian army in pursuit, Napoléon's Grand Army retreats from Russia in October 1812. Thousands of his troops had been killed during the invasion, and those who were left were starving or freezing to death as winter set in. Napoléon's invasion and defeat in Russia were later depicted in Tolstoy's great novel War and Peace.

who did not want to be isolated in Moscow over the winter, ordered a retreat, which turned into a military disaster. Napoléon was defeated by 1814. Aleksandr rode into Paris at the head of his armies and into the councils of Europe. In the search for a more just world order, he created the Holy Alliance of enlightened monarchs. It made Aleksandr an international hero.

Aleksandr did not receive such wide affection at home. Many returning veterans, influenced by the liberalism of the West, tried to make Aleksandr live up to his promises of reform; proposed constitutions were soon being drawn up, and debating societies were formed to promote the ideas of wholesale reform. The reaction from the ruling classes was swift and fierce, and between 1820 and 1825 the state launched a campaign to eliminate the liberal movement. School curricula were overhauled, revolutionary organizations were banned, and subversives were routed. The reign of Aleksandr I ended very differently than it had begun.

Nicholas I

Aleksandr I's unexpected death on December 1, 1825, brought the struggle between the reactionaries and the reformers to a bloody head. It was unclear who would succeed Aleksandr—the late czar's eldest brother, Constantine, or his younger brother, Nicholas. The former did not want the throne, and the latter did not know what to do. Finally, a group of liberal military officers rose up and attempted to force Nicholas into naming a liberal minister to resolve the issue. Nicholas now knew exactly what to do. With the aid of loyalist troops, he crushed the insurrection, hanged several of the plot's leaders, and exiled the remainder to Siberia. Ironically, it was these "Decembrists"— named after the month in which they rebelled—who put Czar Nicholas I firmly on the Russian throne.

The Decembrist uprising clearly had a profound effect on the new czar. Mistrustful of almost everyone, Nicholas favored the lib-

58

An 1830 watercolor depicts a gathering of aristocrats at a Saint Petersburg salon. In December 1825, a group of such aristocrats—mostly liberal, intelligent, patriotic— backed the army officers who revolted against the government. Some of the rebels hoped to establish a constitutional regime, abolish serfdom, and guarantee freedom of press, speech, and religion. Although the revolt was crushed, it became an inspiration for later Russian revolutionaries.

eral notions of his brother Aleksandr but had little intention of allowing them to spread. He could trust the upper class with liberal ideas—they were not a threat to the Crown—and he envisaged an enlightened hierarchy bestowing change upon a receptive people.

While Nicholas instituted cautious reform—laws were drafted that moved toward an abolition of serfdom—peasant riots continued to break out across the empire. Fed up with their dismal plight, the peasants—deeply religious, poorly educated, and indebted to the landlords—forced the more educated Russians into two groups. The Westernizers, composed of mainly young people who wished to bring democracy to Russia, admired the republics in America and France and even constitutional monarchies such as England's. They were tired of the earlier halfhearted attempts at reform. To the opposite extreme were the Slavophiles. They looked back to the days of old Russia, when the czar ruled, the landowners prospered, and the serfs worked. To them, Western ideas were dangerous and threatened the very soul of Russian life.

In 1848 revolution swept Europe. Infected with the ideals of democracy, peoples from Italy to Austria rose up against their leaders in a bid for popular rule. What they received were bloody crackdowns. Revolution did not reach Russia, but fear and loathing did. The government immediately moved against

A Russian cavalry camp during the Crimean War (1853–56), in which Russia suffered a large-scale defeat that worsened the country's political divisions.

the liberals, closing down presses, banning certain books and newspapers, and arresting radical leaders. Whatever degree of free thought had existed in Russia was quickly snuffed out.

Nicholas I died in 1855 a broken man. His reform movement was a failure; his military losses in the Crimea to Turkey, France, and England in 1854 were a lingering humiliation; and the nation was on the verge of political collapse. For the czar, the state of affairs in Russia symbolized a personal defeat, but it represented much more to Russia as a whole: Now the country had lost its middle ground, and radicals and reactionaries were squaring off for a bitter and ultimately decisive confrontation.

Aleksandr II

The reign of Aleksandr II was a turning point in Russian history because of an unstoppable tide of events and Aleksandr's willingness to go along with them. By the time Aleksandr assumed the throne in 1855, the reformist cause in Russia had grown into a revolutionary movement. The world as a whole was changing politically and economically, and autocratic Russia seemed oddly out of place. In America, for example, it was not uncommon for political opponents to accuse their adversaries of being "czarists." Aleksandr realized that Russia had to change before it was too late.

Aleksandr II faced much the same problem that had confronted so many of his royal predecessors. He needed to institute change in order to avoid revolution but could not afford to go too far for fear of creating a conservative backlash. Aleksandr began his rule by surrounding himself with liberal advisers who impressed upon him that the potentially greatest problem facing the country was serfdom. Outbreaks of rioting among the peasants were growing more frequent, and the downtrodden had found an active voice in the intelligentsia—the educated class.

The czar moved quickly. He organized the creation of numerous provincial assemblies across the empire, made up of more than

Czar Aleksandr II assumed the throne in a time of turmoil, when Russia was embroiled in the long and costly Crimean War. Following the Treaty of Paris that ended the war in 1856, Aleksandr promised his people a new epoch of peace—a period of political, economic, and social reform. In 1861, six years after becoming czar, he signed the document that emancipated the serfs.

1,000 representatives of the landowners. Between 1857 and 1859 these deliberative bodies hammered out suggestions to be submitted to the central government, which was determined to overturn serfdom. Finally, on March 3, 1861, a law was approved emancipating the serfs once and for all. According to the law, each landowner had to either rent or sell a plot of his land to each of his former serfs. If the peasant chose to purchase the plot, the government would pay the landowner for the land, and the peasant would then pay back the government over a period of time.

The emancipation of the serfs was undoubtedly the most sweeping reform ever undertaken by a czar; but much to Aleksandr's frustration, the freeing of the serfs seemed only to exacerbate the reigning turmoil. In 1881 the czar himself fell prey to his troubled land—Aleksandr II was assassinated by a small band of violent revolutionaries.

Nicholas II and his wife, Aleksandra Fyodorovna, appear in their court robes in a 1904 photograph. Nicholas, the last czar, was unprepared to rule over the chaotic state of Russia. Eventually he lost both his throne and his life.

5

Revolution and Socialism

In 1894, Nicholas II ascended the throne of Russia and, thanks in large part to his strong-willed, reactionary father, Aleksandr III, the young czar inherited a kingdom on the verge of outright revolution. The embattled landowners were struggling to preserve their way of life; radical revolutionary movements were springing up faster than the police could snuff them out; and the peasants, though free, were seething with resentment because freedom had not brought them prosperity.

Added to this lethal brew was Nicholas's weak character. Upon hearing the news that his father was dead, the 26-year-old prince reportedly cried to his brother-in-law: "What am I going to do? What is going to happen to me . . . to all of Russia? I am not prepared to be a czar. I never wanted to become one." Nicholas's indecisiveness plagued him from the start; he could be readily swayed by persuasive argument, and his domineering German wife, Aleksandra, could influence him at will. (She herself was under the influence of a strange, probably mad priest, Grigory Rasputin.)

But assume the throne he did, and there was much speculation that the new czar would finally bring change to Russia and avert a potential disaster. In fact, many liberals wrongly interpreted Nicholas's nonconfrontational manner as a sign of enlightenment. In another time, Nicholas II would have lived, reigned, and died a monarch who excelled more at sport than government, and he might have been tolerated or even admired as such. But in a time of turmoil he was out of his depth. When confronted with revolutionary rumblings, he reacted instinctively. With the frightened nobility at his side, Nicholas summarily rejected any idea of a true constitutional monarchy and allowed his extensive police force, the Okhrana, to wield considerable power in attacking the numerous pockets of resistance.

He also continued the policy of "Russification" started by his father. By the beginning of the 20th century, the Russian Empire reached halfway around the globe, and the monarchy in Saint Petersburg believed that it could force the numerous non-Russian peoples of the empire to become, in essence, "Russian." Children had to be taught in Russian, the Russian Orthodox church attempted to convert large segments of the population, and organized massacres—called pogroms—were carried out against various ethnic groups, such as the Jews. Though these steps pleased many Russian nationalists, they widened and deepened popular resentment against the throne.

Among those pressing for political change, the liberals constituted the largest group. Some liberals, such as those who supported a constitutional monarchy, sat in the restored Duma, hoping to change the system from within. Others were committed to the idea of a republic. Though continually frustrated in their efforts and often exiled to Siberia, the liberals tended to have the greatest influence because they were generally reformers, not wholesale revolutionaries.

The socialists were a different matter. In 1848, a German intellectual from the middle class, Karl Marx, had collaborated with another young German, Friedrich Engels, to write a short but forceful book, the *Communist Manifesto*. Marx believed that the greed and injustice of the present system of politics would lead to worldwide revolution and the establishment of universal communism. In a communist system the working class would rule, everything short of personal essentials would be owned by the state, and the state would determine the course of society. Marx's untried ideas were extremely attractive to many people who saw no hope in trying to reform the capitalist system of free markets and private ownership.

Marx's ideas became the intellectual foundation for Russian socialism. Russia's Marxian socialists were of numerous minds, but all espoused the idea of total revolution. In 1903, at a party meeting in London, a split developed between two wings of the movement. Led by Vladimir Lenin, the Bolshevik (or majority) wing believed that a small, all-powerful leadership was needed to spark revolution and create a communist state. The Menshevik (or minority) wing, under Georgy Plekhanov, favored a more democratic party with wider membership.

Harassed by the czar's security forces, many of the Bolsheviks, including Lenin, carried out their work in exile; some lower-level party officials, such as Joseph Stalin, instigated rebellion from within Russia itself. Their successes were few. In 1905, a popular revolt shook the monarchy—which, for a brief moment, seemed as if it would collapse—but order was violently restored. In 1906, Pyotr Stolypin became prime minister and, until his assassination in 1911, a degree of pluralism was introduced into political life. However, this pluralism at times bordered on chaos.

The year 1905 also witnessed Russia's humiliating military defeat at the hands of the Japanese Empire. The year before, Japanese forces had attacked Russian positions in Manchuria and later sank much of Russia's Pacific fleet. This drove Russia into a negotiated settlement, mediated by U.S. president Theodore Roosevelt, in which Russia relinquished its holdings in China. Not only did Japan emerge as a world power, but the myth of Russian military prowess was shattered.

As Russia's situation continued to deteriorate, war suddenly broke out across Europe in 1914. Millions of not-so-eager Russians took up arms and marched off to fight the Germans and Austro-Hungarians. The Great War, now known as World War I, was the result of competing alliances and colonial disagreements. It was a struggle of epic proportions, and for the Russians in particular it was cataclysmic. Despite the lessons of Russia's humiliating defeat at the hands of the Japanese, the Russian army, large but ill equipped, fared poorly against the German emperor's forces. By 1916 thousands of cold and starving Russian soldiers simply dropped their arms and went home. To them, it was the czar's war, not theirs.

During the bitter winter of 1916–17, Russia was at the breaking point. Women waited in long lines for food, and heating supplies were scarce. The war was going very badly, for young Russian men refused to go to the front. Meanwhile, the nobility continued to lead a life of luxury, building only further hatred against themselves.

Finally, on March 8, 1917, the czar's world collapsed. The Feb-

The Russian Duma meets in the woods in 1915, during World War I. The war brought not only military embarrassments but also increased pressure on the czar's government. The Duma called upon Nicholas II to replace incompetent officials and end political persecution.

With the Revolution underway, soldiers and civilians are photographed on their way to seize the Duma in Petrograd (Saint Petersburg), March 11, 1917.

ruary Revolution (so called because Russia still used the Julian calendar, 13 days earlier than Western calendars) began when factory workers struck in Petrograd, the new name of Saint Petersburg. As the factory workers poured into the streets, to be joined by students and housewives, the capital suddenly bordered on anarchy. Czar Nicholas rightfully panicked and after two days of demonstrations ordered his troops to fire on the protesters. Some soldiers refused the command, but others obeyed. With blood now running in the streets, Nicholas ordered the Duma to disband. The command was ignored, and the Duma formed a provisional government. Meanwhile, the Bolsheviks had come out into the open and were forming soviets, committees of local workers.

On March 15, 1917, a government delegation visited Nicholas and came away with his abdication and that of his young son, Alexis. The former czar's brother, Grand Duke Michael, refused to assume the throne. After 300 years, the Russian monarchy was no more.

Civil War

For the next seven months, Russia was ruled by a formal provisional government under liberal Duma member Aleksandr

Kerensky. Kerensky represented the more moderate factions in the country. Apart from the monarchists and the Bolsheviks, many Russians believed that this new regime would bring a quick end to the misery of the past two years. Instead, however, Kerensky vowed to pursue the war, in large part because of pressure from Russia's Western allies, who feared a German victory in the east. The economy continued to collapse, men continued to die at the front, and the people of Russia were disgusted.

The Bolsheviks, who viewed the provisional government as little more than an inevitable step toward communism, decided the time was right to act. On November 6, 1917, armed Bolshevik forces launched a coup d'état in Petrograd, forcing the disorganized and confused provisional government to flee. Kerensky himself was whisked out of the capital in the U.S. ambassador's car. The Bolsheviks were now in charge of Petrograd, though not the country itself. They did, however, sign a peace treaty with Germany, the Treaty of Brest-Litovsk, which outraged Russia's allies. The Soviets willingly relinquished many of their western

Czar Nicholas's army mows down a crowd of revolutionary workers in Petrograd, March 11, 1917. Four days later, Nicholas abdicated the throne.

Vladimir Lenin (center left) and Leon Trotsky (saluting), who had led the Bolsheviks in seizing power in 1917, review a parade in Moscow's Red Square in 1919. Lenin had relocated his administration from Petrograd to Moscow in 1918.

territories—Finland, the Baltics, the Ukraine, and Georgia—to either the Germans or to independence movements. The treaty split even the Bolsheviks. Foreign Commissar Leon Trotsky, one of Lenin's oldest associates, resigned in protest, accusing the Soviet state of playing the power politics it professed to despise. Meanwhile, the anti-Bolshevik forces, known as the Whites, began to organize throughout the countryside.

The Russian civil war had begun. The Whites were an assortment of czarists, democrats, militarists, Ukrainian Cossacks, and rival socialists who had little in common besides a collective hatred of the Bolsheviks. The Bolsheviks, for their part, were equally determined to hold on to the power they had seized. Few expected the Bolsheviks to survive, but under the expert hand of Leon Trotsky, the former foreign commissar, the new Red Army was whipped into an effective fighting force. Soon civil conflict had spread to virtually every corner of the empire, and slowly but surely the Bolsheviks gained the upper hand. In 1918, the Western powers sent troops to Russia in an effort to aid the

Whites, but there was little anyone on the outside could do to prevent a Bolshevik victory.

Amid this carnage, the Bolsheviks moved the czar and his family to Ekaterinburg (later known as Sverdlovsk, now Yekaterinburg) in April. In July 1918, Nicholas, his wife, his children, and his aides were herded into a sealed room and killed in a hail of bullets; their remains were dumped in an unmarked grave. The Bolsheviks guarding the royal family had received word from Moscow that a White force was moving toward them and that an attempt might be made to rescue the former czar. Lenin himself may have ordered the executions.

Whatever damage the civil war did not do to the country the Bolsheviks' policies did. Lenin instituted a program called War Communism that placed the allocation of food in the hands of the government. It was a total disaster. The peasants furiously resisted the Bolshevik officials who tried to take their harvests away from them; when the Bolsheviks succeeded, they shipped most of the food to the cities. As a result, Russia was gripped by one of the worst famines in history. A brief border war with Poland in 1920–21 further complicated the situation.

Popular uprisings broke out, and in February 1921 the naval garrison at Kronstadt, just outside Petrograd, launched a failed

In 1921, a Russian family, stricken by the famine that devastated the country after the civil war, rests a while during its search for food.

revolt against the Bolsheviks. Lenin could see that the situation was serious, and he quickly dropped War Communism and even allowed foreign relief agencies into the country. The Bolshevik leader then crafted an economic program, called the New Economic Policy (NEP), that restored a limited free-market system to Russia. Although this pleased many Russians and Westerners alike, Lenin viewed it as merely a temporary measure to be rescinded once stability was restored. Moreover, the NEP allowed for free enterprise primarily at the local level; all industry and banking remained in the hands of the state.

Victory

The capital had been moved back to Moscow, a constitution had been drawn up in 1918, and in 1922 the Union of Soviet Socialist Republics was proclaimed. The civil war was over, and most of the former Whites had either been killed or jailed, gone into exile, or joined the Bolsheviks. Lenin then set out to create the world's first communist state.

The Bolsheviks believed that socialist revolution would soon sweep Europe, and although they were alienated from most of the world, they continued to maintain active ties to foreign revolutionary movements, primarily through the Communist International, or Comintern, an organization dedicated to the overthrow of capitalism. The new government did sign a treaty in 1922 with the world community's other outcast, Germany, and several Western governments, such as Great Britain, which publicly professed hatred of the Bolsheviks, permitted trade with Russia. Many of the world's intellectuals were fascinated with Soviet Russia at this time and actively promoted its ideals and goals.

On January 21, 1924, Lenin, founder of the Soviet Union, died. His death was a tremendous shock to those Russians who had supported him and to the Bolshevik leadership in particular. No one had openly considered a line of succession, and even before

Lenin had been laid to rest, fierce infighting began. The Bolshevik leadership broke into two camps. On one side stood those who continued to support the NEP; with a controlled form of free enterprise, the economy had dramatically improved since the days of famine. On the other side, Leon Trotsky led a minority movement that advocated an end to the NEP and a return to complete socialism—by force, if necessary. The Trotskyists, as they came to be known, also espoused the theory of "permanent revolution." They believed that the Soviet regime's principal objective should be the spread of worldwide revolution. Joseph Stalin, along with much of the party, rejected the idea as dangerous, opting instead to build "socialism in one country." A power struggle ensued, and in 1927 the Communist party expelled Trotsky. Shortly thereafter, he fled the country, never to return. The aging revolutionary was assassinated by a Soviet agent while living in exile in Mexico in 1940.

Joseph Stalin

In the midst of this power struggle stood Joseph Stalin. Born in 1879 in Gori, Georgia, Stalin had spent much of his adult life in czarist jails and was sent into exile in Siberia in 1913 because of his political activities. Later, he served in the upper ranks of the Communist movement by becoming its general secretary. Although he lacked the intelligence and education of the party's top leaders, he made up for these shortcomings with his ability to manipulate others and his violent character. While the party's leading minds were considering the broader issues facing the new Soviet state, Stalin had quietly amassed a personal power base. He would elevate party members to positions of authority so that they, in turn, owed allegiance to him. The general secretary would continually pit one area of the party bureaucracy against another so that no one could grow too powerful. Thus, when Lenin died, it was Stalin who controlled the inner workings of the party, and it was to Stalin that many of the country's lower-ranking officials looked for leadership.

For the first few years after Lenin's death, the country was run by a collective leadership. In the spring of 1928, the first Five-Year Plan was initiated. In this plan the central government set down an economic strategy that depended on agricultural collectivization. The state would take all arable land away from the peasants; they would be expected to work the land as "employees" of collective farms and they would be paid accordingly. Needless to say, collectivization was highly unpopular among the peasants, and resistance was fierce. The Soviets ultimately turned to force to achieve their ends.

By 1928, Stalin was emerging as the paramount leader in the Soviet Union. His power was by no means absolute, however. His greatest threat came from those within the state leadership who had been among Lenin's closest comrades, known as the "Old Bolsheviks." Trotsky was gone, but men such as Grigory Zinovyev, Lev Borisovich Kamenev, and Nikolay Bukharin had known Stalin when he was little more than a glorified clerk. Stalin realized that if he was to survive, he would have to eliminate them.

Whereas other men might have employed political maneuvering to oust their rivals, Stalin turned to wholesale murder. Beginning in 1936, a series of show trials—trials without any legal basis—were held. Day after day, former members of Lenin's inner circle were forced to listen while state prosecutors fabricated accusations of their alleged crimes against the government. Surprisingly, those who stood trial admitted to their supposed guilt. Stalin's lieutenants had used physical and psychological torture to break their victims. The lucky ones were exiled to labor camps, known as *gulags*, in Siberia; most of the Old Bolsheviks were executed.

Soon the Great Purge spread. Lower-level officials suspected of even the slightest hint of dissent disappeared, and most of the military's officers, from generals on down, were summarily tried and executed. And those were just the exterminations reported in the papers. As fear spread, it became common to turn in neighbors, friends, and family to the police. Most such allegations were completely false, but they did save the accuser, if only for the moment. Entire villages were wiped out for being "uncooperative." Untold millions of people died at the hands of Stalin and his henchmen. Estimates of the number killed in the purges have suggested 8 million, 12 million, 20 million or more—the exact number will never be known because most victims were simply dumped into mass graves.

Despite killing so many people, Stalin transformed Russia from a backward agrarian society into an industrial power. Factories produced steel, great dams harnessed the power of rivers, and airplanes and automobiles filled the Soviet Union's skies and streets. Russians enjoyed a new standard of living, and many citizens were thus willing to overlook or justify their leader's barbarity.

World War II

While Stalin continued to terrorize his own people, ominous events were unfolding in other parts of the world. In January 1933, Adolf Hitler, leader of the National Socialist German Workers' (Nazi) party, had assumed the office of German chancellor. The Nazi party was an ultranationalist political movement bent not only upon eliminating Jews, Gypsies, and others they considered "subhuman" from Europe but upon world conquest as well. Hitler believed that Germany should have an empire and that it should be in the east.

Stalin soon realized that Germany was the Soviet Union's greatest threat, and he was determined to do everything possible to avert war between the two countries. His foreign policy shifted three times during the 1930s. The government in Moscow first tried cooperating with Germany against Britain and France,

Germany's two greatest rivals. Then, as Hitler continued to increase the size of his military, Stalin attempted to create an alliance between the Soviet Union, Britain, and France. Unfortunately for Stalin, the Western democracies deeply mistrusted him, in large part because of the Soviet Union's support of revolutionary movements in the West. Finally, on August 23, 1939, after Hitler had marched into Austria and Czechoslovakia and the West had done nothing to stop him, Soviet officials and Nazi leaders stunned the world by signing a nonaggression pact. The world's two greatest ideological rivals were now allies.

On September 1, 1939, Germany invaded Poland, and Britain and France, which had pledged to defend Poland, subsequently declared war on Germany—World War II had begun. The pact between Germany and the Soviet Union allowed the Red Army to invade Poland from the east. Poland had won its freedom from Russia after World War I, and Stalin believed that he was only reclaiming what was rightfully his. Soon the tiny Baltic states of Estonia, Latvia, and Lithuania also succumbed to the government in Moscow, and in the winter of 1939–40, the Soviet Union attacked Finland, another country that had secured its freedom from Russia after World War I. The Finns fought valiantly throughout the winter but were eventually overwhelmed by the huge Red Army.

Stalin was convinced that his cooperation with Hitler was proof that Germany had no designs on Russia; however, on the morning of June 22, 1941, Germany invaded the Soviet Union. Partly because Stalin had killed most of his experienced officers during the purges, the first months of the war were difficult for the Soviets. By the fall, Hitler's forces were within 25 miles of Moscow. The Soviet government had already fled the capital, and it seemed that the regime was on the verge of annihilation. Had winter not set in to slow the German advance, the regime might have been utterly destroyed.

The year 1942 was a pivotal year in the conduct of the war. England had won the Battle of Britain and saved itself from a German invasion, but on December 7, 1941, Japan attacked the United States at Pearl Harbor, Hawaii. With all of the major powers now at war, the Grand Alliance was formed. The Soviet Union, Britain, and the United States banded together in the fight against Germany and its Japanese and Italian partners. American war materiel was soon pouring into both the Soviet Union and Great Britain. While the Soviets turned the tide of battle in the east, the Western allies invaded France on June 6, 1944. On May 4, 1945, Germany finally surrendered, and three months later, after the United States dropped two nuclear bombs on Japan, the Japanese capitulated as well.

During and after the war, Stalin and his American and British counterparts held a series of conferences on the future of Europe. The first conference, held at Yalta in the Crimea in February 1945, was perhaps the most important, for there the world was divided into spheres of influence. The agreements reached at Yalta essentially gave the Soviet Union control of Eastern Europe, its

Soviet leader Joseph Stalin (right) meets with British prime minister Winston Churchill (left) and U.S. president Franklin Roosevelt at Yalta, in the Crimea, in February 1945. At this historic conference, the Big Three, as they were called, decided how the map of Europe would be redrawn after the war.

new "security zone." Germany itself would be temporarily divided between the Soviets in the east and the Americans, British, and French in the west. American president Franklin Roosevelt had hoped that the United States, Britain, France, and the Soviet Union would remain allies after the war, but this was not to be.

The Cold War

As peace settled across the globe in late 1945, the world faced yet another confrontation, this time between former allies. The Red Army was firmly entrenched in the nations of Eastern Europe— Poland, Hungary, Czechoslovakia, Bulgaria, Romania, and the eastern half of Germany—and Stalin had little intention of letting them out of his grip. The Soviets systematically installed Communist regimes that were responsible to no one but the government in Moscow. Democrats were either imprisoned or executed, the free press was abolished, and the borders were closed to the West. The Americans, who had emerged from the war the leaders of the Western world, moved quickly to stem the tide of Soviet expansionism. The Marshall Plan was implemented, giving billions of dollars to help Western Europe rebuild. A Western military alliance, the North Atlantic Treaty Organization (NATO), was formed in 1949, and the Federal Republic of Germany was created that same year out of the three Western occupation zones. On June 25, 1950, Communist North Korea, under Soviet sponsorship, attacked the Republic of South Korea, and the United States led forces of the recently established United Nations (UN) to war in Korea. After three years, the Korean War ended in stalemate, from both a military and a political standpoint.

Stalin took various other steps to fortify the Soviet Union and its sphere of influence against the West. For example, although the German capital, Berlin, fell within the Soviet occupation zone, it was supposed to be divided among all the former allies. In 1947, however, Stalin closed off Berlin to the West. The Western allies responded by airlifting food and other supplies into their part of the city. Stalin eventually realized that he could not pressure the Americans and their allies to leave, and he lifted the blockade in 1948. But he also created the Warsaw Pact alliance, militarily joining the Soviet Union with its puppet regimes in Eastern Europe. In 1953 the Democratic Republic of Germany (East Germany) was formed out of the Soviet zone.

In 1949, the Soviet Union detonated an atomic bomb, making it the second country (after the United States) to possess this incredibly powerful weapon. The United States could no longer threaten the Soviets with a nuclear strike, but neither could the Soviets use the weapon against the West without risking certain retribution. So began the *cold war*—the state of sustained, indirect confrontation between the Soviet Union and the United States and its allies. Their now-indirect struggle—conducted not with arms but with power politics, economic pressure, espionage, and hostile propaganda—soon spread around the globe.

Joseph Stalin died on March 5, 1953, bringing to an end the most brutal period in all of Soviet, perhaps all of Russian, history. The true enormity of his crimes was not immediately recognized; for a time Stalin was actually perceived as a great leader. In 1942, for instance, the Soviet leader was named *Time* magazine's Man of the Year for the second time in three years. Today his tyranny has left him with few admirers.

Khrushchev and Brezhnev

Stalin was succeeded by Nikita Khrushchev, a long-time party official whom Stalin had sent to the Ukraine to help rebuild the devastated region after World War II. Khrushchev, who became first secretary on March 15, 1953, was very different from Stalin. He was short, fat, bald, and given to alternating outbursts of hu-mor and anger, which were falsely rumored to be induced by alcohol. Khrushchev was also a man who had grown to detest the outright barbarity of Stalin; in 1956, in fact, he denounced the former leader in a secret speech to the party.

Khrushchev pursued a foreign policy that attempted to improve relations with the United States while vastly expanding Soviet contacts with the developing nations of the Third World. Beginning with the Communist takeover in China in 1949, communism began to take hold in the poorer countries, in large part because it was an ideology hostile to their former colonial masters in the West. The United States soon found itself helping pro-Western governments and movements in an effort to contain communism. A showdown between the Soviet Union and the United States over Soviet nuclear missiles in pro-Soviet Cuba in 1962 brought the world to the brink of nuclear war. Since the missiles in Cuba were capable of hitting targets in the United States, President John F. Kennedy ordered a naval blockade to prevent the delivery of additional missiles, and the Soviets backed down and agreed to dismantle the missile base. A year earlier, the Soviets had backed an East German plan to construct the Berlin Wall, a physical barrier designed to prevent East Germans from fleeing to the West.

Meanwhile, Khrushchev tried to reform the Soviet Union itself, lessening the state's hold on the economy and encouraging greater freedom of speech. This earned him wide respect from the Soviet people. He also encouraged the Soviet space program and applauded loudest when the Soviet Union launched the world's first space satellite, *Sputnik*, in 1957 and when it put the first man, Yury Gagarin, into space in 1961. But his reform policies, his "defeat" in the Cuban missile crisis, and his embarrassing public displays, such as taking off his shoe and banging it on the table at the United Nations, finally convinced potential rivals that Khrushchev had to be removed from power. In 1964 the

On April 12, 1961, Yury Gagarin, a 27-year-old major in the Soviet air force, became the first human being to travel in space. In the spaceship Vostok *he completed a full orbit of the earth. Here he is seen six days after his historic flight.*

Politburo, the ruling council, abruptly dismissed him from office and eventually replaced him as general secretary with Leonid Brezhnev.

Brezhnev was different from all of his predecessors. The new Soviet chief saw his country not as a revolutionary leader but as a major world power. And the Soviet Union was, by most measures, a superpower. Under Brezhnev the Soviets expanded their conventional and nuclear forces, actively supported pro-Soviet guerrilla movements in the Third World, and initiated what Western commentators called the "Brezhnev Doctrine," a principle of "limited sovereignty" whereby every Communist party was responsible not only to its own people but to all other Communist countries as well. There had been sporadic popular uprisings in Eastern Europe since the end of World War II, the worst of which occurred in Hungary in 1956. Soviet and Warsaw Pact forces had invaded Hungary and restored the despised Commu-

(continued on page 89)

RUSSIAN
AND
SOVIET
PAINTINGS

Overleaf: The Miracle of St. George and the Dragon *(late 15th century) is an icon (a religious image) that was painted on a wooden panel and used in devotions of the Eastern Christians. One of the tales of St. George depicts his struggle with and triumph over the dragon, a symbol of evil. In ancient Russia, St. George was considered to be the patron saint of princes, and in the mid-15th century, the image of St. George defeating the dragon became the coat of arms of Ivan III.*

In Moscow Tavern *(1916), artist Boris Kustodiev has portrayed the everyday life of coachmen warming themselves in a local tavern as they blow on saucers of hot tea. Kustodiev's son later remarked that his father said the painting "makes you think of Novgorod icons and frescos . . . red background, red faces, the same color red walls."*

Entry of the Red Army at Krasnoyarsk in 1920 *by Nikolay Nikonov depicts the welcoming of the soldiers by the exhilarated citizens of Krasnoyarsk. Founded by the cossacks in 1628 and located near gold mines in the region of Siberia, Krasnoyarsk became a center for exiles during czarist times—Lenin himself spent two months there in 1897.*

86

Sergey Gherasimov's Party on the Kolkhoz *(1937), which is exhibited in the State Tretyakov Gallery in Moscow, presents the camaraderie of farm workers during a meal on a collective farm. Before World War II, most people who worked on a kolkhoz were considered to be at the bottom of the social scale, and they often aspired to escape their rural life by moving to the nearest city. However, after the war, village conditions improved and houses and farms were equipped with electricity and running water.*

Marc Chagall (1887–1985), who was born in Vitebsk in western Russia, painted Window in a Dacha *when he and his wife were spending their honeymoon in a small town near Vitebsk in 1915. Beyond the white curtain, the country landscape of birch trees, flowers, and foliage are transformed by Chagall into a simple, tender, and pure symbol of the power of love.*

aaa

(continued from page 80)

nist regime, killing tens of thousands of Hungarians in the process. In 1968 a similar uprising occurred in Czechoslovakia, and in August of that year Soviet tanks rolled in to crush the spirit of an already oppressed people. To justify the action, Brezhnev gave the world his "doctrine," which reserved the Soviet Union's right to lend "fraternal assistance" whenever a "friendly" government was in danger. In other words, the Soviet Union would do anything—including exercise military force—to keep its allies in line.

Although much of the world, particularly the United States, saw the Soviet Union as a threat to global stability, this did not squelch efforts on both sides to reach an understanding that would diminish the threat of world war. In August 1970, West German chancellor Willy Brandt concluded an agreement with the Soviet Union that increased trade and recognized the existence of East Germany. Brandt's policy, called *Ostpolitik* (eastern policy), earned him the respect of Western leaders and the 1971 Nobel Peace Prize. In 1972, American president Richard M. Nixon traveled to the Soviet Union to sign the first Strategic Arms Limitations Treaty (SALT I), which put numerical limits on nuclear weapons. A short time later, General Secretary Brezhnev traveled to Washington, D.C. In 1975, the multinational Helsinki Treaty on European Security and Human Rights was signed, pledging each signatory, including the Soviet Union, to respect human rights. The era of "détente," a French diplomatic term roughly translated as "an absence of conflict," had dawned between East and West, and to many observers it marked the beginning of the end of the cold war.

Over the next several years the United States and the Soviet Union concluded additional arms and trade agreements, but in 1979 an aging Leonid Brezhnev sent a force of more than 100,000 troops to Afghanistan, on the Soviet Union's southern border, to

A poster of Leonid Brezhnev hangs under three of Lenin and one of Stalin at a souvenir stand in Moscow. In their day these men exercised an iron rule over Russia, but by 1995, when this photo was taken, their images were valuable mostly as collectibles sought by foreign tourists.

prop up the pro-Soviet regime. The following year, the Polish government, under Soviet pressure, outlawed Poland's pro-democracy Solidarity movement, and the threat of a Soviet invasion loomed. As the people of Afghanistan and Poland suffered under the weight of the Soviet empire, détente collapsed, and once again the cold war took center stage.

Brezhnev died in 1980, leaving behind a country wallowing in economic and political distress. The growth of the Soviet Union as a superpower had come about at the expense of the Soviet people, whose standard of living resembled that of many Third World nations. Brezhnev was succeeded by former KGB (State Security Committee) chief Yuri Andropov. Though a sickly old man who had built a reputation as head of one of the world's most feared security agencies, Andropov was widely rumored to be a reformer. He elevated several younger men, including Mikhail Gorbachev, to the top seats of power and took tentative steps toward reform. The world never learned precisely what kind of leader he would have been, for Andropov died within two years of taking office. He was succeeded by an even older man, Konstantin Chernenko, who had been favored by Leonid Brezhnev as his successor. Chernenko was also dead within months of assuming office.

The world began to snicker at the Soviets, and the Soviet people began to cringe in embarrassment. Most of their leaders were so old that they could hardly walk on their own, much less rule effectively. But the world soon stopped laughing as a younger leadership, headed by Mikhail Gorbachev, emerged with the professed goal of saving the superpower from itself.

Carrying Moldavian and Romanian flags as well as a picture of Gorbachev, Moldavian nationalists demonstrate in 1989. The repressive Soviet system had curbed aspirations for self-rule among the separate republics of the Soviet Union; but once the central government relaxed its controls, nationalist movements spread rapidly.

6

The Soviet System

To understand the transformation that began to occur in the Soviet Union in the mid-1980s, we must first take a step back to look at the Soviet system that had evolved since the days of Lenin. The repressive patterns of government and society made the nation ripe for a change—and also made that change extremely difficult to achieve.

For most of the 20th century, the Communist party of the Soviet Union was the bedrock of the Soviet state. It had founded the regime, and it gave the government its legitimacy. Lenin and the first Bolsheviks defined the party as the source of all authority and the arbiter of all power. The state was to be its practical extension, and the party's ideals were to be the only source of guidance. The first Soviet constitution bestowed sole political power on the Communist party, and for over 70 years the party was above question in all matters great and small.

Officially, the government and the party were not one and the same, though each was clearly intended to serve the interests of the other. In fact, virtually everyone who served in the government was a party member, making the party organization the true seat of power in the Soviet Union. Lenin defined the party as

94

a ruling elite, and that is how it remained. A party congress was convened every four years to elect the Central Committee, which then elected a ruling council, called the Politburo, and the organizational Secretariat. Traditionally, the Politburo had approximately 20 members, of whom only half were eligible to vote in council; the nonvoting members were referred to as candidates. The true power within this closed echelon rested with the first secretary or general secretary of the Secretariat. Also a Politburo member, he was the supreme leader of the Communist party and, by extension, usually the leader of the Soviet Union as well.

Membership in the Soviet Communist party was always severely limited—only 6 percent of the population belonged—and party members were traditionally the most privileged people in society. Communist indoctrination began at an early age, and schoolchildren were encouraged to join Komsomol, the party's youth league. Those who excelled were taken under the party's wing to be groomed as future leaders. They were sent to the best universities and, if all went according to plan, were allowed membership in the party. Social and career advancement was normally impossible without party membership. The best jobs were given to members, and the best apartments were reserved for their use. Private vacation homes, or *dachas*, located in the countryside or at the seashore, were given to those who rose to

Delegates attend a 1990 Communist party conference in Moscow. Under the Soviet system, party leaders were elected by the Central Committee, which in turn was chosen by regional party organizations.

the top of their profession, whether in government, science, or sports. The party's financial holdings were enormous; it owned resorts and spas around the country for use by its top officials. In a land where most people lived at subsistence levels, those in the party were often granted access to Western consumer goods and enjoyed free trips abroad.

The Soviet Government System

The first Soviet constitution, adopted on July 6, 1923, vested the central government with enormous power. The Congress of Soviets, the supreme ruling body, met once every two years. Daily state operations were the responsibility of the Central Executive Committee, formed from the Soviet of the Union and the Soviet of Nationalities. The Central Executive Committee itself was governed by the Presidium, and it was here that power resided. Because the Soviets were aware of potential national unrest, the first constitution permitted the 15 republics the right to secede peacefully from the union. The first government of the Soviet Union was highly complex, but it was the only way that the Communists could centralize their control without denying nominal representation at the local level.

In 1936 the All-Union Congress of Soviets adopted a new constitution that theoretically expanded democratic representation. Under this new arrangement, the All-Union Congress was replaced by the two-chambered Supreme Soviet, whose members were elected every four years. When the Supreme Soviet was not in session, its Presidium would conduct its daily business. A Council of Ministers was also established. Consisting of experts rather than politicians, its role was to oversee the organs of government.

The government system at the regional and local was a labyrinth of committees, assemblies, and unions. The central constitution called for each republic to have its own system of government, each of which closely paralleled the central structure, and each of which was given a degree of authority over its affairs. Through the Kremlin's pervasive power, though, genuine autonomy was limited, and no action could be taken in any republic without the consent of the Kremlin. The Soviet structure of government also reached down to the workplace and the city block. The soviets, the local political organizations, were the foundation on which the state rested. From these soviets the first state had emerged after the revolution, and it was through the soviets that the Kremlin could control daily life.

After 1936 other changes were made and other constitutions were drafted; still, the often confusing structure that was the Soviet government remained fundamentally unaltered. The Soviets always had the problem of maintaining absolute control while being nominally democratic. The very complexity of the system was an extension of that dilemma.

A Closed Society

The state touched almost every aspect of every citizen's life, whether or not he or she was a Communist party member. Each child's abilities, for example, were gauged at an early age, and the state subsequently determined in what areas that individual might excel. Exhibiting a particular skill as a student could set the course of one's entire work life. The party, the state, and society were intended to be one and the same.

In entertainment and the arts, the state traditionally dictated what people could and could not view. During the 1920s and 1930s, the notion of "socialist morality" became a label for social control. The early Communists believed that permissiveness was a direct result of capitalist "decadence" and that it was the state's responsibility to establish a code of social conduct. This became especially true during the post–World War II era, when rock music emerged as an integral part of Western cul-

The famous climactic scene from Sergey Eisenstein's 1925 film The Battleship Potemkin, *in which innocent civilians are massacred by the czar's soldiers on the long stone stairway in Odessa. By encouraging art of this nature, Soviet leaders promoted the Communist interpretation of Russian history.*

ture. From music to clothing, the Soviets officially banned whatever they disliked.

In art as well, the Soviets determined the norms of acceptability. While they were developing a code of "socialist morality," the Soviets also developed their own approach to art, known as "socialist realism." The Bolsheviks came to power at a time when modernism was being recognized as a distinct art form; for the Bolsheviks, however, it failed to illustrate to the masses the state's ideal "Soviet man." Soviet-approved art was close in style to the realism of the 18th and 19th centuries. The works of such artists as Arkady Plastov depicted Soviet life in all its glory—or imagined glory—complete with heroic Soviet figures bravely defending socialism and happy collective farmers content in their work. This trend carried over into literature, as dramas and novels played on class themes.

Film especially became a vehicle for the state's message. Very early movies, such as the silent film *The Battleship Potemkin*, which glorified a naval mutiny during the reign of Nicholas II, set a precedent. For years after World War II, the Soviet film industry seemed almost incapable of producing anything but melodramatic replays of Soviet victories against the Germans. To most, Soviet "realism" was little more than Soviet propaganda.

Terror

The Soviet state existed as a dictatorship for most of its existence, and it perfected the means for controlling virtually every aspect of society. It is easy enough to control what is written and what is reported, to determine where people can go and what they can do, but it is another matter to harness society itself and transform it into the vehicle of an ideology. However else Lenin's vision of a Communist state may have failed, his plan for an entire society affected by a single political view was, for a time, a wide success.

Lenin's plan was not a total success, though, because the state could never blindly trust the people to follow its lead. Consequently, the element of terror was introduced into society. One of the first measures of power Lenin took when he assumed leadership was to create a security organization—the Cheka—under the leadership of Polish-born Felix Dzerzhinsky. Later known as the KGB (Committee of State Security), this internal police agency enforced the rule of the party at home, destabilized governments abroad, and spied on foreign adversaries. Within the Soviet Union itself, the KGB became an empire within an empire. Through a network of paid professionals and reliable informers, the KGB was capable of squelching dissent in its earliest stages, with a cruelty rarely paralleled. At the height of its power, the KGB was responsible to but a few selected leaders in Moscow—and, reportedly, at times not even to them. The power of the KGB was always extensive, and under the influence of a tyrant like Joseph Stalin it was almost unlimited.

Education, Law, and Social Services

Despite the repressive nature of the Soviet regime, the average citizen did benefit from public services. Health care and educa-

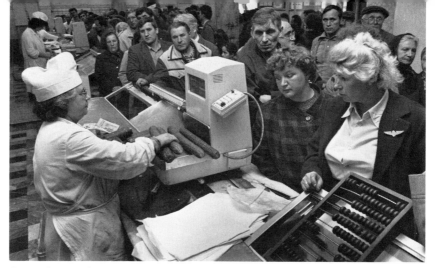

Soviet shoppers line up to buy sausages at a store in 1990. Food shortages were chronic throughout the Soviet Union, and long lines at stores became commonplace.

tion were free, food and housing costs were stabilized, and legal representation was provided by the state. The poor quality of these services, however, often undermined their effectiveness.

Soviet health care on a mass scale was notoriously poor. The country suffered from chronic food shortages; housing was hard to find and generally substandard; the legal system was traditionally an instrument of state terror; and the educational system, though generally quite good, frequently denied individual choice at higher levels. Whatever the relative shortcomings, though, the Soviet people welcomed the regime's giving hand. The Soviets made life less anxious, if no less oppressive, than it had been under the monarchy.

Women

The role of women changed significantly under the Communists. Women in czarist Russia had maintained a status similar to that of their Western peers. Across the social range, women played the traditional roles of wife, mother, and homemaker. Those from the middle and upper classes were educated but were rarely permitted to pursue careers or attain positions of importance. After the revolution, the position of women began to shift. Soviet women received equitable education and responsible jobs, and they were given the same rights as men. They became cosmonauts—the Soviet Union put the first woman into space—scientists, educators, and politicians.

However, as in most other societies, some attitudes toward women were slow to change. Soviet women frequently complained that their men refused to help them in the home. And though at least one woman traditionally sat on the Politburo, a woman never attained a true policy-making position in the government.

Sports

The athletic program became a source of pride and joy for the Soviet Union. Beginning in the 1960s, Soviet athletes became a dominant force in international competition, excelling in hockey, track and field, gymnastics, swimming, ice skating, weight lifting, and tennis. The Soviets regularly ranked near the top at the Olympic Games and in other competitions, including the Goodwill Games. Competitors such as Olga Korbut, one of the greatest gymnasts of all time, elevated Soviet athletes to among the finest in the world.

The Soviets' sports programs were long criticized by much of the international community, however. Amateur athletics practically did not exist in the Soviet Union. As with most of their other accomplishments, the Soviets expended considerable resources to develop their athletics. The best athletes were sorted out at an early age and sent to elaborate training facilities. By the time an athlete reached international competition, sports had become his or her career. Those who achieved greatness were rewarded with homes, cars, and national accolades.

The Need for Change

When the Bolsheviks seized power, Russia was a poor and relatively backward country that had yet to enter the industrial age on a large scale. By the 1980s, the Soviet state was one of the two most powerful military forces on earth. Russians were not wealthy, but neither were they malnourished. The industrial base of the country was slow, inefficient, and highly polluting, but it had become an important part of what appeared to be a formidable economy.

Yet, to many citizens and leaders throughout the Soviet Union, the Communist system seemed unworkable and oppressive. Currents of political opposition began gaining international attention, and the human rights abuses of the Soviet government and its satellite governments in Eastern Europe came under increasing attack. Alcoholism was rampant, and the mighty Soviet industrial machine seemed increasingly unable to produce goods that worked.

Beginning in the mid-1980s, many younger leaders throughout the Soviet Union worried about the deteriorating situation. They recognized that the government had become too bureaucratic, oppressive, and corrupt. Many, if not most of them, wanted to save the Soviet system, not overthrow it. To do so, Mikhail Gorbachev and his supporters proposed to reform the system from the top down. Much of the world supported these efforts, however apprehensively, but few observers could have imagined where they would lead.

In September 1989, the statue of Lenin gestured as commandingly as ever on the main square of Baku, the capital of the Soviet Union's Azerbaijan republic. Below, however, tens of thousands of people were demonstrating in favor of independence from the Soviet Union.

7

The End of the USSR

The fundamental changes that began sweeping the Soviet Union in the mid-1980s have had far-reaching effects. The cold war has ended, and for the first time since World War II, Russia and the West are cooperating in a number of areas, such as arms reduction, trade, and diplomatic initiatives. Russian foreign policy is no longer viewed as a direct threat to the West, and the Russians themselves seem preoccupied with domestic affairs.

The initial changes in the Soviet Union, both foreign and domestic, can be credited to the leadership of Mikhail Gorbachev. Though his rise to power in 1985 signaled the emergence of a younger, well-educated, reformist crop of leaders, Gorbachev singularly personified that enlightened leadership. He gave the reformers a voice and the power they would need to transform the Soviet Union from a stagnant, closed society into a modern state ready to compete in the 21st century.

President Gorbachev was the first Soviet leader since Lenin to hold a university degree and, by coincidence, a law degree as well. Gorbachev demonstrated a genuine respect for the accomplishments of the West. A man of considerable intellect and charisma, he rose through the ranks of the old Soviet system. When he assumed the position of general secretary, Gorbachev was little known outside the Soviet Union. He had earlier traveled to Canada and by all accounts demonstrated a willingness to work with the democracies. But no one could gauge to what extent he was prepared to alter the traditionally hostile relationship between East and West.

Perestroika, Glasnost, and New Thinking

Gorbachev's major concern was the state of the Soviet economy. The Soviet Union was certainly a military Goliath, but its standard of living had never approached that of the West. Basic necessities were always in short supply, and limited quantities of essential products forced people to stand in line for hours outside stores. The quality of consumer goods such as clothing and household appliances was very poor.

Mikhail Gorbachev's intelligence, energy, and charisma drew the admiration and support of many Western leaders. Here, he greets Pope John Paul II during a historic visit to the Vatican in 1989.

Housing was perhaps the most serious problem. The Soviet government was never able to meet the housing needs of the people, forcing entire families to share apartments. Existing housing was often substandard, lacking hot water and private bathrooms.

The reasons for this state of affairs were numerous. The state's ownership of every farm, factory, and store in the country and its insistence on directing the allocation and distribution of every raw material available created a large and inefficient bureaucracy. Lacking any incentive to work hard, the people themselves grew complacent. The deep emotional impact of the Soviet system was evident in the very high rate of alcoholism in the country.

President Gorbachev and his fellow reformers took a dim view of the situation, not only because a world power could not remain one for long with such a weak economy, but also because such crises breed revolt. Gorbachev proposed a series of steps. First, he urged *perestroika* ("restructuring"), that is, the decentralization of the economy and the introduction of limited free markets. Second, he sought an opening of public debate (*glasnost*) through freedom of the press. Finally, he proposed a radical reduction in the Soviet Union's military and global obligations.

The Soviet Union's military and foreign-aid expenditures were enormous. The country maintained the largest overall military machine in the world, with troops stationed in Eastern Europe, along the Chinese border, as well as in Asia, Africa, the Middle East, and the Caribbean. Economic and military aid to its close allies was staggering. Cuba, for example, the tiny island off the coast of Florida, received approximately $5 billion every year from the Soviet Union. Vietnam, India, Nicaragua, and several African countries, including Ethiopia, Mozambique, and Angola, also received large amounts of Soviet aid.

Being a major world power is a costly undertaking. In the case of the Soviet Union, it was potentially bankrupting. President

Gorbachev therefore targeted the military establishment for sharp reductions, but first he had to decrease tensions with the West. Gorbachev's approach to ending the cold war was based on the assumptions that (1) the West had no intention of attacking the Soviet Union and (2) the Soviet Union and the West had enough in common to forge a working relationship. President Gorbachev called this approach to world affairs "New Thinking."

Under the direction of Eduard Shevardnadze, who was foreign minister from 1985 to 1990, the Soviet Union took numerous measures to eliminate hostility and build a sense of trust and cooperation between East and West. This was no small task. Prior to World War II, the stated aim of Soviet foreign policy had been the active overthrow of the democratic-capitalist West and the creation of a global Communist system. After the war and the

Eduard Shevardnadze, the Soviet foreign minister from 1985 to 1990, was a key figure in Gorbachev's overtures to the West. After the breakup of the Soviet Union, Shevardnadze became president of the independent republic of Georgia.

collapse of the Grand Alliance, the Soviet Union's foreign policy became less ideological and more imperialistic. The Soviets systematically subjugated most of Eastern Europe, forged the Warsaw Pact, and tied those pact countries economically to the Soviet Union. As the Third World began to emerge in the 1950s and 1960s, the Soviets exploited lingering resentments against the West in those regions by funding pro-Communist rebel groups and actively undermining the governments in power. Meanwhile, the Soviet military expanded at a staggering rate, and its nuclear arsenal eventually equaled the nuclear arsenals of the United States, Britain, and France combined.

For most of the 20th century, the West had committed itself to preventing the further spread of the Soviet empire. The United States in particular tailored its military and foreign policy to check Soviet ambitions. Occasionally, overtures toward a more cordial relationship were made, first in the late 1950s and again in the early 1970s, but neither side was willing to trust the other. Thus, when Gorbachev began to open the lines of communication with the Soviet Union's old adversaries, most in the West questioned his sincerity, and many Soviets doubted his wisdom.

Two factors greatly contributed to the new Soviet foreign policy. First, Ronald Reagan had won the 1980 U.S. presidential election in part because of his tough, outspoken stance against the Soviet Union. He referred to the Soviet Union as an "evil empire," embarked upon the largest peacetime military buildup in American history, and implored Gorbachev to tear down the Berlin Wall. President Gorbachev realized that any attempt by his country to match the United States militarily might well bankrupt the already suffering Soviet economy.

Second, and perhaps more significant, popular revolt spread like wildfire throughout Eastern Europe in late 1989. The people of Eastern Europe had always harbored a deep hatred of the Communist system imposed on them after World War II. They were aware of how their European brothers lived in the West and resented being subjected to Soviet domination. They had risen up several times before, in 1953, 1956, 1968, and again in 1970, and each time had been brutally suppressed. In each of these earlier instances, revolt had been limited to one country. In 1989, however, East Europeans took to the streets from one end of the region to the other. The Poles had started the process by exacting significant concessions from their government, proving that the Eastern European regimes were not invincible. Faced with the prospect of regional chaos, President Gorbachev broke precedent by permitting—and at times quietly encouraging—these popular movements. By the end of 1989, the Communist regimes of Poland, East Germany, Hungary, Czechoslovakia, Bulgaria, and Romania had fallen, often peacefully, sometimes violently. Democracy had come to Eastern Europe, thanks to Gorbachev's willingness to relinquish the Soviet Union's western empire.

There was now no doubt as to Gorbachev's sincerity. And the Soviet leader continued to make radical changes in his country's world role. He informed many of the Soviet Union's long-time allies, such as Cuba, that his country would no longer be a source of unlimited aid. He joined the West in hammering out diplomatic solutions to many regional disputes—such as those in Angola, Cambodia, and Central America—and rejected many Third World nations' appeals to anti-Western sentiment. In November 1989, Gorbachev did nothing to prevent East and West Germans from toppling the Berlin Wall, and he acceded to popular German and Western demands that the two Germanys finally be reunited, going so far as to agree to a greater Germany's membership in NATO.

The New Revolution: Hopes and Struggles

The Soviet Union was headed down a road from which there was no turning back, mainly because the Soviet people began to enjoy unprecedented levels of freedom. They could elect legitimate representatives, hold their leaders accountable for their deeds, question both the state and its ideology, publish and read what they wished, and express their opinions without fear.

Life under both the czars and the Communists had never been easy; economic and physical suffering without the freedom to stand up for one's inalienable rights had a profound impact on the people of this vast land. The outside world, in fact, assumed that the Soviet people had somehow resigned themselves to a life of quiet misery. All that changed dramatically. The Russian people put their leaders and the world on notice that they were neither content nor willing to accept a future similar to the past.

Accepting this change, the government systematically stripped itself of much of its power, admitted its past mistakes, and made peace with the world. The Soviet Union was undergoing nothing less than a revolution, complete with all the hopes and fears that are part of every great upheaval.

By 1990, some of the dangers of this revolution became apparent. A number of the Soviet Union's smaller republics began to assert their independence, to the dismay of most in the central government. Ethnic tensions and civil disorders were increasing. The economy, loosed from its shackles, was stumbling in its transition to a Western-style free market. Politically, Russian society had split into two warring camps, the reformers and the reactionaries, neither of whom were content with the country's apparent downward slide. President Gorbachev gradually found himself on the defensive, accused both of not moving far enough fast enough and of leading the country toward total collapse. Gorbachev's political skills had traditionally served him well, allowing him to keep his feet in both camps while steering a middle course. But the country's economic and social problems, plus the anxieties of party and military leaders, finally forced Gorbachev into taking sides.

Thousands of Lithuanians demonstrate for independence in the streets of the capital city of Vilnius in August 1989. Such "nationalist hysteria," as Soviet leaders termed it, worried the Kremlin and soon led to Soviet military attacks against Lithuania and Latvia.

Reformers could sense Gorbachev's wavering commitment to change, but it was not until December 20, 1990, that their fears were confirmed. In an impassioned speech before the Soviet parliament, Foreign Minister Eduard Shevardnadze, an architect of Gorbachev's New Thinking, abruptly resigned his post, arguing that the country was sliding into a new dictatorship. President Gorbachev, who had asked the Supreme Soviet for expanded powers to help him deal with the spiraling economic and civil strife, was shocked and insulted by his long-time ally's speech.

The meaning of Shevardnadze's message became clearer when, during the last week of December, the Congress of People's Deputies voted to give Gorbachev absolute control over the executive branch of government and authority to rule by decree if necessary. In addition, the Congress confirmed Gorbachev's choice for first vice-president of the Soviet Union, Gennady Yanayev, a conservative party bureaucrat. Many understood these developments as signaling the dictatorship of which Shevardnadze had spoken.

The Soviet Union Crumbles

Gorbachev's former domestic allies continued to watch as conditions deteriorated by the day. On January 13, 1991, Soviet tanks plowed into a crowd of hundreds of unarmed nationalists in Lithuania's capital city of Vilnius. Fifteen people were killed and more than 100 were wounded. After the attack, the National Salvation Committee, a shadowy pro-Kremlin group wishing to overthrow the elected, independence-minded Lithuanian government, seized the broadcast facilities and television studios in Vilnius and claimed to have taken over the city. The Soviet army's sudden show of force was the largest there since Lithuania had declared independence nearly one year earlier. Lithuanians and their Latvian neighbors, who were themselves attacked shortly thereafter, quickly formed civilian militias, declaring that they would rather die than capitulate to the Kremlin.

Emboldened Soviet newspapers immediately lashed out at Gorbachev, blaming him for the army's violence in the Baltics. Gorbachev responded by calling for the suspension of press freedoms. At first unwilling to answer the question of who had given the order to open fire on civilians, Gorbachev later claimed that it was not the Kremlin but local military commanders who had taken action. He went on to blame the Baltics' separatist leadership itself for bringing on the bloodshed by leaving the military no choice but to apply force. He then renewed his call for press censorship during such crises.

Gorbachev's strong-arm tactics accelerated as the month wore on. In an effort to crush the thriving black market, Moscow suddenly announced that citizens had only three days to exchange their 50- and 100-ruble notes for smaller bills. Large ruble bills were a mainstay of the black market. At the same time, the Kremlin announced that the army would patrol the streets of major cities jointly with local police forces in an effort to control a growing crime wave. Days later, President Gorbachev invested the KGB with extensive powers of search and seizure.

Soviet reformers, and much of the world, were perplexed by Gorbachev's slide toward dictatorial rule. Many observers believe that hard-liners from the military, the KGB, and the party gave Gorbachev an ultimatum: Either restore order or step down. If this was the case, then Gorbachev had lost his political free will. However, it is often forgotten that Gorbachev's original calls for perestroika and glasnost were designed to improve the existing order, not to overthrow it. Gorbachev himself, therefore, may have grown intolerant enough of the resulting chaos that he instinctively moved to crack down on dissent.

In August 1991, Communist hard-liners placed Gorbachev under house arrest and sought to reverse the reform process. Reformers, led by Boris Yeltsin, who had become president of Russia the previous month, managed to crush this attempted coup, but then they immediately began to dismantle what remained of the Communist party apparatus. Gorbachev resigned as general secretary of the Communist party. As the Soviet Union approached a total disintegration, a new transitional government, headed by Gorbachev, was established on September 5. The new State Council recognized the full independence of Latvia, Lithuania, and Estonia.

As president of the largest republic in the Soviet Union, Boris Yeltsin began to exert greater influence, and the Russian government quickly assumed the powers of the Soviet government. Yeltsin proposed to replace the USSR with a Commonwealth of Independent States, which would be open to all of the republics in the Soviet Union. The Russian parliament approved the plan, and on December 12, Ukraine and Belarus joined Russia as cofounders of the new union. Eight other former Soviet republics (Armenia, Azerbaijan, Kazakstan, Kyrgyzstan, Moldova, Tajikistan, Turkmenistan, and Uzbekistan) were admitted two weeks

A complex figure, Boris Yeltsin showed as much charisma as Gorbachev, but of a very different kind. Here, he appeals to young people by dancing at a rock concert.

later. The republic of Georgia joined the commonwealth in 1993. Latvia, Lithuania, and Estonia declined to join.

The USSR had effectively ceased to exist. On December 25, 1991, Mikhail Gorbachev submitted his resignation as president of the Soviet Union. Russia assumed the seat on the Security Council of the United Nations that had been occupied by the USSR, and the UN admitted the other newly independent states to membership.

The sudden transformation was one of the most stunning and dramatic events of the 20th century. At the time of its collapse, the Soviet Union encompassed over 8.5 million square miles, and it was home to nearly 300 million people. The old system had been a failure, and few mourned its loss. For the people of the new Russia, the road ahead held many promises, but also many difficulties.

A girl sits on a Moscow street in 1992 with a kitten for sale. As the Russian economy struggled in its attempted transition to capitalism, sale of family pets became an all-too-common phenomenon.

8

Steps Toward the Future

Two primary factors contributed to the breakdown of Soviet society and government. First, Gorbachev's policy of perestroika—the restructuring of the economy—actually led to worsening economic conditions. The reformers were intent on introducing a free-market system in which private citizens could own the factories, stores, and farms. The transition from a state-controlled economy had never been tried before on such a large scale. Perhaps not surprisingly, it produced widespread shortages of such basic necessities as bread, potatoes, and fuel. Furthermore, as the government moved to close unprofitable state enterprises, many people lost their jobs. Homelessness became widespread. The people grew angry and afraid and held their leaders directly responsible for the deteriorating situation.

Second, the Communist party had fallen into complete disrepute. As the mechanism that had held the country together for seven decades, the Communist party suddenly appeared impotent. The people openly blamed the party, its socialist policies, and its wide corruption for ruining the country. Yet no political force emerged to replace the party and prevent the complete breakdown of central rule. Consequently, one republic after another declared its independence from the party and the government.

For the West, one of the most nagging questions was what, if anything, should be done about the rapidly deteriorating situation in the Soviet Union. Gorbachev's early reforms had earned him almost mythical status in the West, and Western policymakers had placed much of their hopes for a new, less aggressive Soviet Union on this one man. Hence there was much inclination to help Gorbachev survive his crises. But critics warned that, should Gorbachev fall from power or permanently change direction in his policies, the West's new relationship with Moscow might well fall by the wayside. Others said that assisting Gorbachev would only serve to prop up a dying Communist system, the system against which the West had struggled for so long. When Gorbachev shifted in an authoritarian direction, the critics appeared to have been right. Still, no one seemed certain of who could take his place. The West mostly watched, anxious and fascinated, as the Soviet Union dissolved and Boris Yeltsin emerged as the head of an independent Russia.

The Yeltsin Presidency

Boris Yeltsin, like Gorbachev, was a long-time member of the Communist party. Gorbachev was responsible for elevating Yeltsin into prominence by placing him in charge of party operations in Moscow in 1985. But Yeltsin quickly made many enemies in that position, and he was removed from the post in 1987. He became a popular political figure in the late 1980s and early 1990s in part because of his criticisms of Gorbachev and other Communist leaders. In June 1991, riding that popularity, Yeltsin was elected president of Russia—a position that within months made him the head of an independent state.

Following the dissolution of the USSR, Yeltsin initiated a program of radical economic reform in Russia, promoting Western investments and free markets. But opposition to such steps remained strong in the Russian parliament. The parliament obstructed most of Yeltsin's principal initiatives, such as drafting a new constitution, preparing new elections, and launching economic and political reforms. Yeltsin fought back. In April 1993, he sought and received a vote of confidence in a national referendum on his leadership and economic policies. Two months later he convened a constitutional conference, which drafted a new constitution for Russia.

Fed up by the continuing political stalemate, Yeltsin dissolved parliament in September 1993 and called for new national elections. His opponents in the legislature tried to instigate an armed insurrection the following month by occupying the parliament building, but Yeltsin ordered the army to respond forcefully. The president prevailed, and immediately he banned opposition parties and newspapers.

Smoke rises from the Russian parliament building in October 1993 as troops loyal to President Yeltsin suppress an armed revolt by legislators.

In December of that year, Russian voters elected a new parliament and approved the new constitution that had been drafted in July. The voting further established Yeltsin as the dominant political figure in Russia, but it also demonstrated significant opposition from across the political spectrum. Ultra-nationalists, liberals, communists, and agrarians all gained substantial representation at all levels of the Russian government.

At the root of the political disputes was the worsening economic situation. Yeltsin and the economic reformers claimed that the parliamentary opposition was largely to blame for dragging its feet on restructuring the economy. Many of Yeltsin's opponents argued, in turn, that he was trying to accomplish too much, too fast, and that a deeply entrenched economic system could not be uprooted overnight. Furthermore, suspicions were intensified by reports of widespread corruption at the upper levels of government and industry. Many figures in and around the government were reported to be amassing huge fortunes through questionable financial means. While the disputes continued, life for the majority of Russians was growing more and more difficult, with hunger, homelessness, and unemployment all spreading throughout the country.

In late 1994, Russian troops invaded Chechnya, a republic in southwestern Russia that had declared its independence in 1991. Yeltsin's decision to reclaim the republic was seen by many as an indication that Russia wished to discourage other separatist rebellions among ethnic groups in the area around the Caucasus Mountains. For the next year and a half, Chechen and Russian troops fought a bloody conflict in which the Russian army used heavy weapons against civilians and committed other brutal acts. More than 40,000 people were killed, including large numbers of civilians, and over half a million were displaced by the war.

To many observers, the Russian actions in Chechnya seemed

puzzling and raised serious concerns about the intentions of the new Russian leadership. Within Russia itself, the media and large numbers of citizens actively opposed the war effort. Yeltsin's popularity, at home and abroad, declined sharply. In legislative elections held in December 1995, the largest vote went to candidates of the Communist party, who captured more than one-third of the seats in the State Duma. The Communists, led by Gennady Zyuganov, sharply opposed Yeltsin's free-market reforms and offered a more nationalistic approach to foreign policy. The extreme right-wing Liberal Democratic party, led by the ultranationalist Vladimir Zhirinovskiy, finished second in the voting. Prime Minister Viktor Chernomyrdin's Our Home Is Russia party was third.

Yeltsin's popularity had seemingly never been lower. Moreover, there were persistent concerns about his health. Yeltsin was hospitalized twice in 1995 for a heart condition (which would eventu-

A Chechen woman salvages belongings from her home, destroyed by a Russian air raid in December 1994.

The resurgence of Russian ultranationalism in the 1990s was represented most forcefully by Vladimir Zhirinovskiy of the Liberal Democratic party, seen here campaigning in 1993.

ally require bypass surgery in November 1996), and his frequent disappearances from public view led to speculation about his condition and who was ruling the country. He was also rumored to be a heavy and self-destructive drinker. Nevertheless, he announced his intention to seek a second term as president.

In the June 1996 elections, neither Yeltsin nor his primary opponent, the Communist Gennady Zyuganov, received 50 percent of the vote, forcing a runoff between the two in July. Yeltsin won with nearly 54 percent of the vote. A month later, he won reprieve from another crisis when Russian and Chechen authorities finally negotiated an agreement. Russian troops withdrew from Chechnya, and Chechen elections were held in January 1997. By May 1997, the two sides had concluded a peace treaty and agreed to reach a final settlement by the year 2001.

Government Today

The constitution that Russian voters approved in 1993 provides for a democratic government composed of three branches that exert checks and balances over each other. The executive branch consists of an elected president as its chief, with a government headed by a prime minister. Boris Yeltsin was elected to a five-year term as president in 1991, but beginning with the 1996 elections, presidents serve a four-year term. The Russian constitution allows for no vice president. If the president can no longer exercise the powers of the office, the prime minister becomes acting president until new elections can be held. Viktor Chernomyrdin became prime minister in 1992.

The bicameral legislature—known as the Federal Assembly—

Russian Communist party leader Gennady Zyuganov speaks at a press conference in 1996. Though it had fallen into disgrace in the early 1990s, the Communist party rebounded strongly as the Russian economy stumbled. In the June 1996 presidential election Zyuganov forced Boris Yeltsin into a runoff.

consists of the State Duma and the Council of the Federation. The highest body in the judicial branch is the Constitutional Court, whose members are appointed by the Federation Council at the recommendation of the president. The Supreme Court is the highest court for criminal, civil, and administrative cases. The legal system is based on civil law, allowing judicial review of legislative acts. Although it is nominally independent, the judiciary is often manipulated by political authorities. Large backlogs of cases and lengthy pretrial detention remain serious problems.

The Russian Federation, as the country is formally known, is composed of 21 autonomous republics plus the federal cities of Moscow and Saint Petersburg. The leaders of the republics form the Council of Heads of Republics, which is part of the executive branch. Leaders of the 66 autonomous territories and regions, plus the mayors of Moscow and Saint Petersburg, form the Council of Heads of Administrations.

The Economy

Russia would seem to have most of the vital elements of a healthy and productive capitalist economy: It is a large country full of natural resources, a diversified industrial base, and a well-educated population. Even so, the transition from the centrally planned economy that marked communism to a market economy has been especially difficult. The breakup of the Soviet Union also destroyed the complex, if inefficient, economic system that had become entrenched over the course of its existence.

Yeltsin's government launched its economic reform program in January 1992. Controls on the prices of most goods were eliminated, defense spending was reduced sharply, foreign trade and the distribution of goods were freed from centralized control, and state-owned industries began to be privatized. The promised benefits of these changes have been slow to develop. Many Russians believe that their condition has worsened rather than improved since the collapse of the Soviet system. Real wages in fact have fallen, unemployment has grown, and corruption and crime have become widespread social concerns. Industrial and agricultural production consistently declined through the mid-1990s, and the health of average Russians was measurably worse because of a deteriorating diet and problems in the health care system. By the start of Yeltsin's second term as president, millions of citizens were going without paychecks and pension payments, and according to official statistics, over 25 percent of the population was living in poverty.

The strong showing of Communists and nationalists in the elections to the State Duma in 1995 reflected the extent of popular dissatisfaction and made the economic transition all the more difficult. In recognition of the problems facing his economic reforms, in March 1997 President Yeltsin reorganized his cabinet to strengthen the position of liberal reformers and speed up economic change. Yeltsin asked for the resignations of all cabinet members except for Prime Minister Viktor Chernomyrdin and First Deputy Prime Minister Anatoly Chubais. The Russian bureaucracy was also streamlined through the elimination of several ministries and a reduction in the number of high-level posts.

Trade

A primary motivation for the reforms launched by Mikhail Gorbachev was the Soviet Union's need for expanded trade with the West. The West had long been reluctant to trade with the Soviet Union for two reasons: First, there was a concerted effort to keep high technology out of the hands of the Soviet military. Computer technology, in particular, is critical to a modern army, and Soviet computers were generations behind those of the West.

Second, Soviet currency, the ruble, was nonconvertible; that is, it could not be traded for Western currencies because it was not based on a universal standard, such as gold or silver. In essence,

Soviet money was worthless in the non-Communist world. This meant that the Soviets had to acquire Western goods either by paying with hard currency, such as gold, or by swapping something that the West needed. But the Soviets had only a limited supply of gold, and their consumer goods were generally inferior to those of the West. Trade, in other words, faced many roadblocks.

Adding to the problem in the late 1980s was the collapse of traditional trade relations that had existed between the Soviet Union and Eastern European countries. As those countries broke away from Soviet control, they began forming their own economic relationships, largely with countries in the West. Consequently, by the mid-1990s, the volume of trade that Russia conducted with foreign countries had fallen well below its level of ten years earlier.

Russia's new leaders made strenuous attempts to revitalize trade, as well as a concerted effort to encourage Western investment in Russia. Western partners would bring the capital, technology, and know-how that the country needed so desperately. A 1992 trade agreement between Russia and the United States provided for mutual most-favored-nation status. The United States has also actively supported Russia's efforts to join the World Trade Organization (WTO). Few people expect a rapid turnaround in the Russian trade situation, but Russian leaders have continued to predict improvement in the near future.

The Environment

Along with its economic and trade difficulties, Russia has some severe environmental problems. Much of the air, water, and soil have been polluted, largely because Russia's heavy industries and mines were constructed with little if any concern for environmental controls. Even agricultural production has long relied on the heavy use of chemicals.

For power, the country is heavily dependent on coal-fired electric plants and poorly designed nuclear reactors. The 1986 explosion at the Chernobyl nuclear plant in Ukraine, which killed 31 people directly and spread radioactive material across a wide swath of Europe, was a major embarrassment for the old Soviet regime. Today, the condition of nuclear plants in independent Russia is far from reassuring. One of Russia's most important industrial centers, the city of Chelyabinsk in the southern Ural Mountains, may be the most radioactive place in the world because of spills and discharges from its plutonium plant. In encouraging new economic development, the Russian government will need to take care to avoid the environmental carelessness of the past.

Foreign Affairs

Although U.S. president Bill Clinton soon became perhaps the most outspoken supporter of Boris Yeltsin among Western leaders, important problems between the two nations persisted. Of particular concern for the Russians has been the U.S. commitment to expand membership in the North American Treaty Organization (NATO) to include former Soviet-bloc nations. For years, NATO stood in opposition to the Soviet-inspired Warsaw Pact. With the dissolution of the Warsaw Pact in 1991, some considered NATO's mission to be over as well. Others argued that NATO was needed to control instability in eastern Europe and to continue solidifying post–cold war relationships in the area.

At a March 1997 summit with President Clinton, Yeltsin reiterated Russia's opposition to the expansion of NATO. Two months later, however, Russia reached an agreement with NATO that appeared to clear the way for NATO's expansion into central and eastern Europe. In July 1997, NATO formally invited the Czech Republic, Hungary, and Poland—all former Soviet allies—to become NATO members.

The U.S. space shuttle Atlantis *(below) docks with the Russian space station* Mir *in 1995. Joint space missions became a well-publicized symbol of increasing cooperation between the two countries.*

Meanwhile, Russia has taken steps to find new allies in the region. In April 1997, President Yeltsin and Chinese President Jiang Zemin signed a joint declaration pledging renewed cooperation. The declaration was an important step in restoring relations between Russia and China that had been bitter for decades. Trade between the two countries is expected to increase dramatically. China imports weapons, nuclear technology, and industrial goods from Russia in exchange for inexpensive food and clothing. Russian leaders have also sought to strengthen ties with Iran, India, and Belarus.

On important international conflicts, Russia has become an

important mediating force. It was a co-sponsor of the Middle East peace process and supported initiatives in the Persian Gulf, Cambodia, Angola, the former Yugoslavia, and Haiti. Russia also contributed troops to the NATO-led stabilization force in Bosnia.

A new Russian military doctrine, issued in 1993, called for a smaller military with regional, as opposed to global, ambitions. Implementation of this new doctrine has not been smooth, however. The resulting cutbacks in military spending have been severe, producing reductions in training, long delays in payment to troops, shortages in housing, and reports of a serious decline of military morale and cohesion. Many observers saw evidence of these problems in Russia's poor combat performance in the Chechen conflict.

Along with the size and scope of the military, weapons production in Russia has fallen dramatically since the late 1980s. Most of the weapons now produced are intended for sale to foreign governments. Many defense industries have collapsed, adding to the nation's economic woes, while others have been privatized.

The Road Ahead

Today, Russia is a vast country with deep contrasts and ironies. The streets of the capital, Moscow, seem to be full of new luxury automobiles, and the skyline is being transformed by modern office buildings. Vast amounts of wealth are being accumulated, mostly in the sometimes murky transactions by which state-owned companies are being transferred to private ownership. Yet, throughout the countryside, Russia remains trapped within perhaps the most widespread economic depression in the past century. In 1996, fully 75 percent of Russian farms lost money. It is estimated that small family plots provide half of all food produced in Russia, a statistic that illustrates the extent of the country's decline into a subsistence economy.

New wealth has yet to be funneled back into productive investments that could create jobs and lead to economic growth and prosperity. And foreign investment, although it has been rising a bit in some sectors, has not come close to reaching the level that Russian leaders feel is necessary for the country's future. Foreigners invested a mere $2 billion in Russia in 1995. By contrast, China received nearly $38 billion in foreign investments.

Predictions, by Russians and foreigners, of what the future holds are wildly inconsistent: Many see Russia becoming a booming industrial giant once again, this time with an economy resting on free trade and backed by a democratic political system. Current economic problems, they argue, are a necessary, yet temporary prelude to growth and prosperity. Others argue that Russia has begun sinking into the status of an overgrown Third World country, a former superpower that entered the world capitalist economy too late to establish its own solid foundation.

Most views fall somewhere in between these two extremes. What is not in dispute, however, is that the fate of millions of Russians rests on crucial decisions to be made in the coming years. The whole world will be watching with concern, hoping that Russia finds its way to a peaceful and stable prosperity.

GLOSSARY

balalaika   A traditional six-stringed triangular instrument resembling a guitar.

Bolsheviks   Translated as "majority," this is the name given to those Communists led by Lenin who broke with their fellow revolutionaries in 1903.

boyars   The landowners who ruled at the regional and local levels during the reign of the czars.

Council of the Federation   The upper house of the Russian legislature.

détente   A French diplomatic term loosely translated as "absence of conflict." It most commonly refers to the period of cooperation between the United States and the Soviet Union during the 1970s.

Duma   The council of the boyars that officially shared power with the czars and local land councils.

Federal Assembly   Russia's national legislature.

*glasnos*t   Translated as "openness," this was the name Gorbachev gave to his program of encouraging free speech and popular debate.

Komsomol   The Communist party's youth organization.

perestroika	Mikhail Gorbachev's program of economic renewal; literally, "restructuring."
ruble	The Russian currency.
Sobory	The local land councils that officially shared power with the czars and the council of boyars.
soviets	The local cells of workers formed by the Bolsheviks before the 1917 Revolution and retained afterward.
State Duma	The lower house of the Russian legislature.
ukaz	An official edict handed down by the czar.
Zemsky Sobor	An "assembly of the country" composed of the boyars (landowners); also referred to as "the Sobor." The initial Zemsky Sobor elected Ivan IV as the first czar in 1549.

INDEX

PICTURE CREDITS